Praise for Kate and *Exposed*

Becoming "set free" took incredible strength for Kate to break out of her invisible cage that was her reality. She speaks from her heart as a truth seeker and redeemed survivor of a reality that most people never want to think about. Thank you, Kate, for revealing to us the life of bondage that, unfortunately, so many women find themselves trapped in. Get ready for your eyes be opened so that you might be allowed to have a part in women being rescued from the darkness to the light.

Becky Allender, co-founder of The Allender Center at The Seattle School of Psychology and Theology; author of *Hidden In Plain Sight: One Woman's Search for Identity, Intimacy and Calling.*

Kate is as real and true as they come! She boldly shares her story in hopes that you, dear reader, will feel seen and known in your own experiences. She stands today as a living example of the fact that we can not only survive the trauma of our past, but we have the capacity to *overcome* it. If you need a reminder that you are not alone, and encouragement that you too have what it takes to live a life of wholeness and freedom, then this book is for you!

Harmony Dust, MSW, author of *Scars and Stilettos: The Transformation of an Exotic Dancer*; founder of Treasures.

I met Kate at a therapist-led support group years ago when she first started sharing her story with others. I am so proud of who she has become. I think this is a great resource for those who are or have been in the sex industry. It provides thoughtful questions for you to answer at the end of each chapter, so it really gets you thinking. I highly recommend this book!

Crissy Outlaw, former porn actress and support group facilitator

Kate has always struck me as one of those people who has earned every bit of the boldness, softness, power, and welcoming acceptance she exudes. Like the saying goes, "No one will know the violence it took to become this gentle." *Exposed* is an important work of art that embodies both the profound pain and profound purpose that can come from surviving the sex industry. Her life continues to be a testament to the value and strength inherent in all people when we find voice, courage and community to empower ourselves and others.

Rachel C. Thomas, M. Ed., human trafficking educator; appointed member, United States Advisory Council on Human Trafficking

Kate is the hero of her own story but also on behalf of other lost and exploited women. The sex industry is a vicious consumer of goodness, innocence, and agency. Loss of agency because one is forced to make choices from other bad choices creates a powerlessness and a hopelessness few escape from. Kate did. She was born with a fierce tenderness that evil could not devour, although it tried. She not only survived horrors most only imagine or watch on television, but she built a life for herself, had a beautiful family, and went on to start Cherished, a non-profit organization providing resources for women caught in the trap of sexual exploitation and empowering them to recover their voice and agency to build a life worth living.

This book should be in the hands of every follower of Jesus because He goes into the darkness to find the Lost One. Kate was that one, so was I, so are you. Risk looking into the fragmented face of this beautiful survivor and find a way to love these women through Kate's brave story. She's risking everything to write this book and put it in your hands. Steward it well. You're reading a sacred, holy story, of a woman who loves much because she has been forgiven much. May you leave these pages altered by her story, as she was, and never again look away from the faces of women used and abused by the sex industry. Kate is a warrior for the oppressed. She is MY hero too.

Rhonda Reynolds, story midwife, www.RedeemingtheTable.net

Kate's writing is gritty and soulful. She indeed exposes the systemized commercial sex industry first-hand, but she also shares vulnerable stories of innocence, goodness, and hope. Kate's story carries the universal theme of longing to be chosen and the deep well of betrayal. As a survivor, it nearly cost Kate her life. Knowing her personally, I can testify that Kate's words come from a profound place of truth and integrity.

Natalie Sum, LPC

The International Labor Organization (ILO) estimates that there are currently 25 million victims of human trafficking around the world. In her book, *Exposed*, Kate Wedell takes the reader inside this evil empire of exploitation and abuse and gives us a terrifying first-hand account of being lured, trapped, and controlled. Journey with her as she fights to escape this living prison and eventually finds healing.

> **Cyndi Mesmer,** LCPC, founder & co-owner of The Art of Living Counseling Center, in Crystal Lake, IL; founder & CEO of Equity Bridge, a non-profit organization bringing the equity gap of marginalized communities

I write as someone who knows and has worked with survivors of sex trafficking. I know firsthand the absolute terror they experience when they take the first step towards restoration. I know how much it takes for a survivor to deaden her internal self in order to keep going. The thoughts of suicide and self-harm that have taken up residence in her mind. The climb out of sex trafficking is one that I do not think anyone but a survivor would understand. And yet, that is what Kate has done. She has climbed out of the world she was once pulled into. She has faced evil and continues the fight to not only live, but to live fully. Here she offers us pictures…the graphic details of being in 'the life'. *Exposed*. She exposes what she knows many would prefer not to see. She offers her words with the greatest of courage and vulnerability in the hopes that others, those on the journey, will find hope. Kate has scaled Mt. Everest and she has conquered and continues to conquer the path of growth and healing.

> **Corinne Vance,** licensed psychotherapist working with those who have experienced sexual violence and exploitation; partnered with The WellHouse in Odenville, AL, The Seattle School of Theology and Psychology; on the leadership team of International Christian Alliance on Prostitution (ICAP)

Through a fearless and compassionate lens, *Exposed* unveils the hidden and often misunderstood world of the commercial sex industry and domestic trafficking. An eye-opening exploration into a realm that society often chooses to ignore, this book delves deep, challenging preconceived notions and revealing the intricate web of circumstances that clutch and cage individuals into this life. Kate, the author, paints a mosaic of raw emotion, resilience, and human connection, urging readers to not only bear witness but to question and, most importantly, truly understand. A pivotal read for anyone seeking insight into this labyrinth of dark corners within society, *Exposed* takes a letter opener to the dirty nailbed of the game and its players.

Cory James, founder & CEO, Words of Hope

In *Exposed: Surviving the Commercial Sex Industry*, Kate Wedell takes you on an unflinching journey through the harrowing world of sex trafficking, but this time, with a remarkable twist. Kate's powerful narrative brings to light the unimaginable horrors faced by those ensnared in the commercial sex industry, yet it goes beyond that. With unwavering compassion and a profound commitment to healing, she provides a beacon of hope for survivors yearning to reclaim their lives.

Through her own lived experiences, she'll guide you, revealing the strength, resilience, and unbreakable spirit of survivors who have defied the odds. Explore the intricate path towards healing and transformation. *Exposed* is not just a book; it's a lifeline for those seeking solace and a chance at a brighter tomorrow.

This groundbreaking work doesn't just expose the darkness; it illuminates the way out. Join in on this extraordinary journey of survival, redemption, and the indomitable power of the human spirit. *Exposed* is a testament to the unwavering belief that healing is possible, even in the face of the most profound trauma.

Armand King, author of *Raised in Pimp City*

In her groundbreaking memoir *Exposed*, Kate de Varennes Ouimette-Wedell invites us into the depths of her harrowing story of trauma, survival, resilience and liberation. With unwavering courage and fierce kindness, she offers an unfiltered account of her ten-year bondage in the commercial sex industry, illuminating the horrific realities that so often remain cloaked in shadow. Shedding light on the nuances and complexities of escaping a life many cannot comprehend, she calls on all of us to be allies in the battle against exploitation.

This book is not merely a story to be consumed, but a beacon of hope for those who find themselves longing to be liberated from the clutches of the industry and a clarion call for action. Kate's generous vulnerability of both her suffering and her recovery provides such stunning imagination for healing, rebuilding and the gospel promise that God will bring beauty from the ashes of our pain. What a profound labor of love.

Rachael Clinton Chen, director of teaching at The Allender Center and Co-Host of the Allender Center podcast

Kate has given us the gift of seeing the resilience she has carried throughout her childhood and adult life. Her story has made me believe again in the hopefulness of healing. Her desire to help herself by helping others is breathtaking. She has a way of telling the truth that is setting her and others free, and sometimes facing the truth is harder than living the horrors of an unprotected childhood. Kate has fought hard to tell the truth and begin to let her body heal from the deep scars of trauma it has held over a lifetime. Her tenacity and will to not only live but to truly heal is the most hopeful thing I've witnessed. She is a true queen.

What struck me the most was that no one ever came looking for her. That heart break alone is crushing. Then I realized, in the end she came looking. That is true resilience.

Christine Flynn, trauma coach, story sage, friend;
http://www.thestoryhouse.info

She slipped a piece of paper in my hand after I was done speaking at the youth group. It had Kate's name and number on it and went on to say 'Call my mom! I think you two would be great friends!' And guess what? She was right!

I've known Kate for thirteen years. We've shared a lot of laughs and a lot of tears. Kate is a keeper of stories: she knows mine (all of it) and I know hers—a true friendship. To write an unedited version of your life story for the whole wide world to see takes a kind of courage that most people don't have. Kate is brave and has that kind of courage. What compelled her to continue in the process of writing *Exposed*, even when faced with countless obstacles and adversity, was her big, beautiful, and genuine love for the girls in the sex industry. Kate was in the sex industry, and CherishedLA was birthed out of a deep desire for what Kate wished was available to her during that time. The book you hold in your hands is her living, breathing account of some of what led her into and out of the sex industry.

The message she has lived since I have known her is, 'You are loved, valued, and cherished, and this book was written as a lifeline of hope for women who want to believe in something better and to those of us who want to make a difference.' As Kate always says, 'You never know what part of someone's healing journey you are in.'

I've watched Kate work hard in the process of her own healing, willing to go to the deepest parts of herself, as painful as it was, to find freedom and wholeness. Her book is filled with incredible wisdom and counsel for those who have experienced the trauma of the sex industry. She gives back a voice to tell their stories and guide them forward so they can dream again.

There is no greater love than to lay down one's life for one's friends. This book is the laying down of Kate's life. Raw and vulnerable, bringing beauty from ashes!

Karen Fish

Kate Wedell is both incredibly brave and brilliant in this well-written exposé of her life and struggles in and out of the sex industry. I have had the privilege of working with Kate in the fight to abolish the sex-trafficking of women and children and am in awe of her resilience, her commitment to true freedom, and her incredible transparency. She has taught me the reality of what society calls 'the choice of a woman' in an industry that is nothing short of slavery to a male demand. She has taught me that freedom comes at a cost, and the rewards of fighting for the freedom of others. Kate's journey is a beacon of light to those who are trapped in the same cage but also a call to action for those of us who can't turn a blind eye and look the other way. I can't recommend this book enough; it will open your eyes and put a fire in your belly to be part of the solution. We are all called to protect our women and children, every single one of us!

Sally Cook, author and co-founder of Hope Refuge

The seven years I have worked alongside Kate have been some of the most profound years of my life. I am deeply honored for the ways that she has shared her journey with me and the trust that she has extended. It is the same trust that she is extending to each of you in writing her memoir, *Exposed*. It is a deeply vulnerable experience to allow others into the stories of your life, as Kate does in these pages. It is something I have seen her do often with other survivors, allowing them to see both the stories of her younger self and the ways she is still healing.

Kate is one of the most courageous, compassionate, Christ-filled people that I know. She loves fiercely, with open hands, encouraging each survivor (and person) she knows to discover more of themselves and the depths of their own heart. I am truly grateful to her for the ways that she has seen me and allowed me to see her. I am also filled with gratitude for the trust she has extended in allowing me to walk alongside survivors at Cherished.

Many well-meaning people end up doing more harm as they find themselves face to face with powerlessness through the stories shared by survivors. Witnessing Kate's approach, I have seen the immense well of love and compassion that she has. I have also witnessed her deeply attuned sense for when and how to speak painful truths and how it allows survivors to finally be free to name and grieve those harms. To each survivor reading this, I know that you will be safe and seen in the pages of this book. And for everyone else, I hope that as you read it, you will do so knowing that you walk on sacred ground. There is healing here for you, too, if you have the courage to see yourself in these pages.

Kayla Campbell, executive director, CherishedLA

EXPOSED

EXPOSED

SURVIVING THE COMMERCIAL SEX INDUSTRY

KATE **de** VARENNES OUIMETTE-WEDELL

Printed in the United States of America.
First paperback edition November 2023.

Cover and layout design by G Sharp Design, LLC.
www.gsharpmajor.com

ISBN 979-8-9894254-0-2 (paperback)
ISBN 979-8-9894254-1-9 (ebook)

About the cover: I knew I wanted something that signifies how fragmented those years were for me, when looking in the mirror it was hard to see clearly who I was anymore. I saw a fashion photo somewhere like this and it immediately struck me. The image spoke so deeply to how I felt, I knew my cover must convey the same. It took many different talented people tweaking it to get the exact cover that I was looking for.

Thank you so much to:
Erica Herron, Red Jacket Photography
Ellie Wedell, Film Editor
Printopia
Kayla Campbell, E.D. CherishedLA
Kristine Estes, Moonwalkerdigital.com
Cory James,
George Stevens, G Sharp Design LLC

You nailed it!

Published in Los Angeles, California, by Cherished Publishing. Cherished Publishing tells the stories of survivors of trafficking and exploitation.

To all survivors.

FOREWORD

By Trapper Lukaart

If you have picked up this book there is a good chance you fall into one of two camps. You are a woman that knows first-hand the profound exploitation and abuse that is the backbone of the sex industry, or you are a person that is unwilling to turn a blind eye from the millions of girls and woman suffering under its oppressive appetite. Most everybody else has brushed up against some element of the sex industry – internet pornography, that one bachelor party, news of sex trafficking rings – enough to offer a snapshot, but one short of the full view when the curtain is pulled back. With an unflinching honesty, Kate offers us precious, heartbreaking, ultimately hopeful stories of her life and their convergence with a dark, predatory industry.

The stories that most shape who we are or redirect the course of a life are rarely the easy or pleasant stories. We are marked most deeply by our personal stories of heartache and tragedy, and they reside in us, just below the surface of our consciousness while having a say on nearly every aspect of our lives. So often these are the stories that do not get told; it takes hope and courage to pull them from their hiding places, and a deep desire for meaning and freedom to tell them.

I first met Kate at a workshop in Seattle where people gathered to tell their untold stories; stories that shame and that polite society would prefer to remain locked in the basement and out of sight. It is an oddly hopeful and resilient collection of people that fill the rooms of this workshop, and Kate was no exception.

Within minutes of meeting Kate, it was evident that she would not fit neatly into any standardized social box. She is composed yet earnest and intense. Funny and whimsical, with a finely tuned BS meter. She is quite capable of small talk on a broad array of topics, but she is far more likely to cut to the heart of the matter. I liked her immediately. She approached me at this conference with what was essentially a job offer, though working with her instead of for her.

The job was to travel with and occasionally guide, in the endeavor to understand and make meaning of the interplay of life events, relationships, and her internal world. The primary context of our relationship was the psychotherapy office. There are a great number of paths to a therapist office, but the most common theme is that some form of personal or interpersonal pain has become too much of a hinderance to ignore. Inasmuch as pain awakens us to seek healing and change, I am grateful for its motivational properties.

Kate, however, was one of the rare exceptions. By the end of our first session, it was clear that she hadn't located herself on my cliché brown leather sofa to find relief from something—not primarily, at least. Instead, she was running toward something and was willing to overturn any and all the stones of her life in service of understanding and truth; and ultimately to be free to love more fully.

Though the transformative work Kate invested herself in was for her, she also carried an inherent understanding that if the stories of her life remained in the dark, some part of her would be conceding to the dank shadows that the sex industry and shame rely on to continue to profit from degradation.

She was running toward something
and was willing to overturn any and
all the stones of her life in service
of understanding and truth.

...

Kate offers us the shaping stories of her life, and in the telling of these stories she exposes the true face of the sex industry. Crucially she debunks any remnants of the myth that women freely choose to enter and then remain in the sex industry without harrowing circumstance and profound trauma in childhood and early adulthood guiding the way.

Every transaction in this dark industry – and their numbers are staggering – involves a person that has been stripped of power and made into a commodity in service of violent and sexual appetites that can never be satiated. For so many women, literal survival in the sex industry depends heavily on developing a protective exterior, a persona that can interact with those holding the power and the money. Soft-heartedness, true desire, and even love—these are liabilities that must not be exposed to those propping up an industry that prizes the annihilation of innocence.

Mistaking the presentation of a necessary persona for a woman that is empowered and free to choose is a grave error.

Kate is indeed a survivor, but the term by itself does not adequately capture the grit, resilience, and hope that are central to a survivor's character and choices. Emerging from the industry as a survivor is as much a beginning as it is an ending, and this precarious nexus is where Kate has committed much of her life's work. Escape and recovery are certainly linked but they are far from the same thing.

Cherished is the apt name for the non-profit organization she founded over a decade ago to help women rediscover both themselves and a path away from the sex industry. Built into the ethos and practice of Cherished is the gentle invitation for women to experience the liberating, terrifying practice of exposing one's vulnerabilities, desires, and innocence in a place where it can be met with kindness and belonging. The antidote to the brutal impact of the exposure demanded from the sex industry is the exposure of one's true self and heart. Throughout the pages of this book, we get to witness a rare interplay of these vastly different kinds of exposure.

Without claim of expertise or "arrival," Kate has a keen understanding of the terrain that funnels women into the sex industry. More importantly, she knows intimately, the cost, compassion, and courage to be free of it by telling the full, complicated truth.

Though there are many trauma experts, the only true trauma sherpas that can help guide others through and to the other side are those that have traversed the range of their own heart and body in search of who they are most meant to be. You have such an expert guide in this author.

LETTER TO YOU

Dear Survivor,

I wrote my story for the two of us, you and me.

I tell it with boldness on behalf of you and all the women who haven't yet found a safe place to be vulnerable. I know how lonely it is to live with the feeling that most people will never fully understand what you have seen and endured.

I tell these stories for both of us, because you need a witness to all you have been through. Your story matters, your voice matters. The things you have experienced have been horrific, and those things need to be named and grieved for what you have missed.

For so many years I was all alone suffering from C-PTSD with no one to talk to. It seemed like no one would be able to handle my story, so I walked around carrying the shame of feeling like I was always too much or never good enough.

I tell these stories for me because I needed to write them, to know this was real. I needed to get closure on the things that have haunted me and held me prisoner for 26 years.

I want you to know these stories are my past. It has been a long journey for me.

I am grateful for what my life, my stories, have taught me and how they have played a huge role in who I am today. Someone who knows what it's like to fall and get back up again and again. Someone who knows what this healing road looks like. Someone who is finding freedom and who is discovering with each new day who I truly am and what my life is meant to be.

What you have experienced is more than most people will ever understand.

You are not crazy.

You are not too much!

You are not who they said you are.

You are stunning!

There is no one like you!

You are worthy of honor and goodness

and you are worthy of being truly loved.

My hope is that you will find yourself in these pages no matter where you are on your journey and realize that you are not alone.

There is HOPE for so much more!

And as you read my stories, you are my witness, and I am not alone in it anymore either.

Thank you!

Kate

To everyone else,

If you have picked up this book, you need to know something before turning the page. This book is written for those who have experienced life in the sex industry. You may find yourself offended, shocked, aroused, or afraid that I have crossed a line. But I have not.

I have written every word for those who can relate to the experiences in this book; they will not be shocked by this content. I have written to offer a face that doesn't turn away when others do, because their story might be too much for someone who has never entered this space to be able to hold.

If you do not identify as a survivor of the commercial sex industry or are not currently working in the sex industry, this book was not primarily written for you. If the raw truth about the sex industry, the set up, and the sexual abuse it is, shown under the magnifying lens, is too much to process, then please feel free to put this book down now. It's okay.

However, it is my hope that if you decide to read what is written in these pages, then you will do so with an open, teachable heart; to see how childhood events and sexual abuse are a direct correlation to set someone up for a life in the sex industry, and how the trauma of it follows you without proper healing in those areas.

I pray that after reading my story you will learn to have curiosity and empathy to walk alongside others who are suffering from trauma; to recognize that sexual harm is not a "choice" or "empowering," but a result of something so much deeper.

It's time to humanize those who have been dehumanized for the lust of others.

TABLE OF CONTENTS

PART 1

CHAPTER 1

AN INVISIBLE CAGE

"How many more nights like this would
I have to endure before I would finally
get what I had come to LA for?"

. . .

I sat in the backstage dressing room at the strip club, getting ready for my next set.

The night was still early; all I could think of was going home. This felt like it was going to be another one of those long nights.

From the looks of it, there were no signs of any big tippers in the crowd, just those who came to look while paying the very minimal price of the cover charge. I knew if I didn't make enough at the club tonight, I would have to take "calls" to make up for it, making this night even more excruciating. But the possibility of ending up homeless was very real and not something I was EVER going to let happen again!

Already it was turning out to be another night of the same old song and dance. Literally.

The other dancers all played the same songs for their sets almost every night, and frankly, I was tired of hearing the "stripper soundtrack": White Snake, Bon Jovi, Motley Crew, and so on.

I would choose songs I could escape into, and I would dance! R&B old school and current dance music was my main thing; Mothers Finest (*Baby Love*), Tina Marie (*Starchild*), Zapp & Roger, SOS, KC & The Sunshine Band, En Vouge, Tina Turner (*Whole Lotta Love*, such a great song), Janet Jackson, Prince (*House quake!*), George Clinton (*Atomic Dog)*.

A Taste of Honey, The Spinners, Earth Wind and Fire, and The Ohio Players—I made sure to pick songs from almost every genre; Grand Funk Railroad, Stevie Ray Vaughn, The Cure, Enigma, Lenny Kravitz, Santana, Nine Inch Nails, Aretha Franklin (*Chain Of Fools*), Sting (*Sister Moon;* my favorite song to this day!), The Church, Echo and the Bunnymen—the list goes on and on.

It all depended on my mood that night, the costumes, and the clientele. Music usually made me come to life, but not tonight. Tonight, everything seemed to be moving in slow motion, and the music didn't help.

I had no idea if showing up at work tonight would be worth the effort or just another night lost in time. It was always unpredictable. One thing I could count on was what awaited me when I would finally return home.

I had decided to get a pet—something for companionship so I wouldn't be so alone, something that could survive if I was away too long—so I purchased two small, beautiful, snow-white doves. They were my only sense of "normalcy;" my only companion and comfort. I would let them out of their cage to fly around my room freely whenever I finally got home after working a long night. I understood how it felt to live in a cage, longing to be free.

Sometimes I would turn on the shower in the bathroom and watch them tilt their little heads, listening for where the sound was coming from. When they finally discovered it, they would perch under the water with their wings spread like they were standing under a waterfall, allowing the water to wash over them and clean their beautiful white feathers. They were so lovely and graceful yet delicate.

I imagined they longed for the real thing.

I understood how it felt; I, too, wanted to be free from my invisible cage.

I could relate to them standing under the running water as long as they could.

I, too, knew the relief of standing in the shower for what seemed like hours, never feeling clean enough, wanting the water to wash it all from me...the night, the men, the smells.

It was life-giving to be around something so beautiful and innocent.

My reflection in the dressing room mirror came back into view as I stared in the mirror at my make-up and the glitter; I wondered how many more nights like this would I have to endure before I would finally get what I had come to LA for?

QUESTIONS: AN INVISIBLE CAGE

Take some time to think about this (and be really honest) before you answer these questions. I suggest doing this book as a group and sharing your answers at the end of each chapter in a group discussion—you will be surprised that you are not alone and it helps to have others eyes on your story or you don't have to. It's your choice. But I do recommend taking things that come up for you to a good therapist that understand complex PTSD. (If you need help finding someone, I have a list of where to get started in the back of this book.)

Our reflections can show us a lot.

1. Is there something in your life that you have done that you named as a "choice," but if you're honest with yourself, you really didn't want to go through with it and you felt there was no other way?

2. If there had been an option, would you have "chosen" something else?

CHAPTER 2

WELCOME TO LA
(FLASHBACK)

"I was literally going to be homeless
if he didn't help me, and he knew it
and used it to his advantage."

. . .

My entire life, I had been dreaming about going to California and pursuing my dreams of being an entertainer in the music business. Not just dreaming but a deep longing like a homesick feeling that hung over me. Our language doesn't have a word to describe how deep a sense like this resides in the soul, so I will borrow it from one that does. Saudade. It's Portuguese. I learned it in Brazil. It describes that sad longing for something missing or absent. California was that for me. I would literally watch the sunset out my window on the east coast and think of that same sun shining bright on the west coast beach while night was swallowing my world. That's how my life felt. Depressing and absent.

I finally got a taste of the life I wanted, singing and traveling with a band for a year, but that was over now. For as much as I had been on stage with the band, I still had a lot of fear. I was always trying to hide how uncomfortable I felt in my skin. I was scared of what people were thinking of me, fearing their judgment of my talent, afraid I might not have what it takes to make it. Whenever I told someone what I was going to do, they would always say, "you definitely have the look." But I felt something was missing, and that haunted me.

I felt something was missing, and that haunted me.

...

 Singing on stage feels like being naked in front of strangers. You are completely exposed. You're vulnerable. People can see all of you, and they judge.

One night someone at the recording studio asked me if I was really sure LA was for me; what was I waiting for? When was I planning to go? I didn't really have an answer. If not now, when?

I started thinking it may never happen if I kept waiting around. So, I decided to just do it!

I knew there was one person that could help me. An Italian restaurant owner (apparently involved with the mafia and from NY) that was always asking me out.

He was usually dressed in some designer suit, typically white, and always had an entourage of beautiful women around him. The champagne poured freely at his table, and he always promised some fancy "next time" if I would come be with him, which he made good some of the time.

This time, though, was different. I was just returning from being on the road. I didn't have very much money or anything of value to sell, only the car that he had helped me get.

I let him know I was in town for a night and, sure enough, he asked me to have dinner with him.

I never wanted to be "his girl;" he was too arrogant and rude. He just wanted people around to worship him, and he had a temper when he didn't get his way. I could only take that kind of narcissism in tiny doses. But I knew I could get what I wanted if I played my cards right. And I knew how to do it and escape his clutches just in time. I knew he wanted to be my "sugar daddy," but I had too much dignity for that. I just had to stay one step ahead and make sure I kept the ball in my court. When I said yes to dinner and drinks, my plan was to convince him to buy back my car from me, and I wasn't leaving until he agreed. Then I would have the money I needed. That was it. This was just a business deal. That's all I wanted.

But instead, he saw this was his chance to make me bend to his will.

I didn't want to stay that night with him, but he said "no deal" if I didn't. I needed to get away from this town, this dead end I was in. There had been too much pain here, and I felt like he was my only hope if I wanted to get out to LA. I was really disappointed there were strings attached. I was hopeful he'd take me seriously; this wasn't a game for me. This was my life. But this time, I couldn't get around it; a transaction was obviously being made, and we were discussing it upfront. He was finally putting me in the role of the escort he wanted me to be. He knew how badly I wanted to go to Hollywood. Now my dream came with a price—and out of necessity, I agreed to his terms.

When I left his place the next morning, I knew I'd never return.

I didn't waste a moment. I bought a one-way plane ticket to LA for the following day! When I got the ticket, I couldn't stop looking at it. This was gold to me. My way out!

I couldn't believe this was finally happening for real. Inside I was screaming! *THIS was the biggest moment of my life! This was "my dream come true"!!!*

I had never been out of the South, and now I had a plane ticket, a little money, and a friend to stay with in Hollywood.

Steve, who I knew through many late-night recording sessions, had now moved to LA. He had always told me that he was going to, and he'd say, "if you ever come to LA, call me, and you can stay with me." We had worked together for a while back then, always staying up late doing coke and laying down tracks. Sometimes mine and sometimes for Fred (Funki).

Anytime I was in town, Fred and I were together, and he and I would often end up over in the recording studio. Fred was my true love (although I never let him know) and when I was with him I was the happiest. I knew we would be doing what we both loved! They had heard me talk of going to LA and now Steve was actually going and inviting me to come see him. "When you come to CA, at least you'll know someone there now. Just call me!"

I had always thought about it like, "Yeah, one day…" But this time, when I thought about it, there was nothing holding me back, except fear. Okay! I'll do it! Why not? He'll be waiting and show me around, we'd reminisce, and I would have some protection, someone safe to check in with who could show me the ropes.

Listen, you don't offer a southern girl hospitality in a foreign place, ESPECIALLY one that she has DREAMED about going to her WHOLE LIFE!!!

I felt lucky to have a friend in LA who was in "the business." I felt like this must be destiny; it was the perfect, safe opportunity to take the leap!

The day after selling my car, I boarded the plane with everything I owned in two suitcases. On the flight, I was so excited; this felt unbelievable! I had so much hope for my future! It's the only explanation for how I could muster up the courage to go the farthest I had ever been away from home to a place where I had nothing and no one. But at least I had one friend out there. That was the one thing that helped me decide that now was the time to go. I stared out the window of the 747 as we took off. I could feel the wheels leaving the ground. I remember thinking, "I am never coming back here."

I was finally going after my dream! My thoughts returned to my Italian friend, who had manipulated me over the car. He easily could have just bought it back from me and gotten any of his many employees to take it and make payments to him to get it off his hands. It was really no skin off his back. I thought he'd show me more respect. After all, I hadn't been in town hangin' out like one of his trophy girls. He knew I was leaving to pursue my career. I had been on the road as a lead singer, following my dreams. But to talk to him about buying my car, I had to play the game, have dinner and stay with him that night. At first, it was somewhat flattering to be asked to dinner by him, to be the one chosen. So many were always trying to get his attention. He could wine and dine you and make you feel special. So I decided dinner that night would serve two purposes. It would also be my bon voyage party, even if I were the only one celebrating. And it was. Sort of.

I watched the clouds under the plane's wings and thought, "Well, I can put that behind me now, and at least I won't have to deal with him anymore. And I was leaving behind all the drug dealers. It was all in the past; I was starting over, and my future was bright!

When I landed in LA, it felt like a dream. I pinched myself. I was so EXCITED!

I went to a pay phone right away and called Steve.

"Hey! You made it! Welcome to LA, sit tight. I'll be there soon, just wait at the bar, and I'll come get you." So I did. I waited. An hour went by, and then I called him again to see when he was coming.

"Ummm, I'm stuck in this recording session right now," he said. "Can you take a cab over to the studio? It's in Hollywood." I said sure, trying to be brave. I don't think I had ever taken a cab alone. I didn't even know how to get one. But I was getting restless at the bar in the airport, so I asked the bartender where to get a cab. Anytime I had flown it was from small airports in the South, and someone was always waiting to pick me up. This was the first of many new adventures, and I was excited to see Hollywood!

I thought "Wow, he's doing great, maybe he's with someone famous that I will get to meet if I get there in time. I didn't think about it then, but our recording sessions back when I worked with him would go long into the night, too, often into the early morning, and the only time he would take a break was to get more cocaine. It took every penny I had left from selling the car to get a cab from LAX to Hollywood. I felt embarrassed to show up with my luggage to the studio, but what else could I do? It probably looked like something you'd see in a movie scene. Cut to a young, naive Southern girl, who comes to Hollywood to make it big, goes straight to the studio with a suitcase in hand, expecting to get her big break! I never expected that to be my first stop when I arrived in Hollywood.

I was very excited! The studio was huge! Even though it was late, there were still sessions going on, and even though I was exhausted, there was no place that I would rather be. I didn't mind at all spending my first night in the recording studio. After waiting for him to finish the recording session, it was almost sunrise, and we went to his apartment. I crashed hard on the couch. I woke up when I heard a girl's voice. She sounded pissed. It was his girlfriend. She had stopped by, and I guess he hadn't told her about me coming. When she saw me there, she told him that he had better kick me out. It was her or me. Our relationship had always been totally platonic – I was in love with Funki – and Steve tried to tell her how we knew each other from back home, but she wouldn't believe him. Steve walked in the room and said I couldn't stay with him anymore.

I was shocked he would do this to me, and I was terrified! "Please let me stay," I pleaded with him. "I don't have anywhere to go! I don't know anyone else in LA, and I don't have money or any family to call that will help me." Can't you talk to her, please?? I begged.

I was literally going to be homeless if he didn't help me. I was entirely at his mercy, and he knew it. He used the situation to his advantage. He was still "using," and I could have never imagined how bad it had gotten. He made a phone call, and the next thing I knew, he was loading my suitcase into his car and told me to get in. We drove away from his apartment in silence, neither saying a word. Hot tears rolled down my face. Just twelve hours ago, I was ecstatic, having more hope and joy than I had ever known on my way to the studio in Hollywood, and now I felt more scared than I had ever felt. There was literally no one to call there to help me. I couldn't believe a friend could be so cold. We arrived at a three-story house set in the Hollywood Hills that rose above Grauman's Chinese Theatre.

A guy stepped out to meet Steve and me. He looked at me and smiled, and I smiled back, hoping he was a nice friend who would let me stay in one of the rooms until I got on my feet. He looked like a regular working guy. I hoped he would tell me I could rent a room there and pay him after I got a job. Instead, the guy handed something to Steve, who then quickly pulled my luggage out of the car and drove away fast. That was the last time I ever saw Steve. I didn't realize it then, but my value had just been reduced to an eightball of cocaine. In just a few hours of arriving in this magical place I had dreamed of, I had been traded for drugs. Sold. I was trapped, and I had no one.

I didn't realize it then, but I had just been sold for an eight-ball of cocaine.

...

We went to the third floor to his room. He left for work, and I cried for the rest of the night until I fell asleep on the futon at the foot of his bed. I assumed we were alone in the house, but the next day I discovered another woman lived there, too, on the second floor. I only saw her a few times, and we didn't talk. She was older, and so I assumed she was the owner of this mansion. I had no idea how many rooms were in the house, but there were so many I didn't see all the doors. She had cats in many different rooms and some of the closets. They were separated into groups. I was forbidden to open doors to any of the rooms. I'm still not sure why. I was confined to one room on the third floor unless I had to leave the house to go to work. The rest of the house was off-limits to me. I didn't have any money for food, so the only time I ate was if the guy brought home leftovers from his dinner. Sometimes I would sneak downstairs to the kitchen when he was gone and look for a piece of bread or even a cracker. If I got caught, I got yelled at and called a thief, threatened to call the police, or throw me out on the street if she saw me down there again.

I desperately wanted to leave the house. In the mornings, I'd wake up hearing chanting noises. I didn't know what this was about or meant. At night, I was expected to show my gratitude for having a place to stay by performing sex acts with him. Survival sex. Instead of coming to the promised land to find my dreams, I was in hell. I felt sick all day and night.

Trapped. Betrayed. Desperate. Alone.

My plan was to get into a good salon and find a roommate to start with, but I needed time to make this happen. My North Carolina cosmetology license wasn't valid in California, so I would have to apply for a new one, but that meant having a permanent address and money to get the paperwork taken care of and find a model for the exam, and I still didn't know a soul. I prayed to God I could find something more permanent soon and that I would not still be at this house in six months. I would need to get a job to tide me over until I could get a California cosmetology license so I could get into a salon, but in LA, even to get a waitressing job in a good restaurant, you needed headshots and to get headshots you needed money. I had never had headshots or the cash to get them. I was used to being lonely, but this was different; I was isolated and so far from home and my familiar surroundings. I had crossed my own boundaries and fallen further than I ever imagined. But I knew there was no turning back or calling home for help. I had gotten myself into this situation, and I would have to get out somehow and figure it all out myself... like always.

Needing money, fast, I decided to apply for a dancing job in a bikini bar. When I arrived for my audition, I felt sick. It was mostly an after-five bar with construction workers. There wasn't even a DJ, just a jukebox that the customers fed with quarters, or the bartender would put money in it to keep it going if no one else played a song when it was silent for too long. It felt ridiculous wearing a bikini and stilettos in a small dive bar with a small square wood floor I would hardly call a stage.

The music I selected started playing, but I was too paralyzed to move. I don't even remember dancing, but my garter was full of money by the time the song ended. I just remember trying to act like I was wearing regular clothes. The money wasn't as good as I had hoped it would be. Friday was about the only good shift in the bar. The energy was better because it was payday for most of the customers, and the *cervezas* were flowing, which helped as far as making more tips. At some point, though, when the customers had too much to drink, the money would cease, and instead of tips, you just got crude and vulgar propositions.

I got to know the girls in the dressing room, and I quickly realized that strip clubs were full of girls who wanted to break into the modeling, movie, or music business. Other girls said they were just stripping for the money; it was only temporary, and they had bigger dreams for themselves. But after a while, I could see their plans fade, along with the opportunities for anyone to take them seriously. I didn't want this to happen to me.

QUESTIONS: WELCOME TO LA

In this chapter I decide to pursue my dream of coming to LA. I knew this was my destiny and longed for it since early childhood, but when I decided to go for it, it became my nightmare.

1. Have you ever had a life dream? What was it?

2. Have you ever been betrayed by a friend or someone you thought you could trust?

3. What has "survival" cost you?

CHAPTER 3

WHAT'S YOUR NAME?

"Finding out who you really are is much harder
than creating who you think you need to be."

. . .

When you were given your name, whoever named you probably had something or someone in mind. It could have been a tribute to someone they respected, or maybe it was a name passed down as a family tradition. Your name probably had a special meaning.

Before I was born, my dad had hoped I'd be a boy. He planned to name me Miles, I assume after Miles Davis, the great jazz musician, because he was also a musician and loved jazz. Instead, I was born a girl, and my parents named me Kate, which means "pure." A nod to my mom's Irish heritage. My middle name, deVarennes, means "of a symbol" and was the name of my father's (French) grandmother.

The meaning of my full given name is "a symbol of purity."

Women in the commercial sex entertainment industry either willingly or by force change their names to separate themselves from real life and create a pseudo-life. Slave owners did the same thing. After buying a slave, the owner would change their name so that he could "break them" by stripping them from their roots. It's no different in the sex industry. Human Trafficking is called modern-day slavery for a reason, and this is just another example of how it all works.

I've worked with hundreds of survivors, and I've traveled in many parts of the world and talked to women working in brothels and on the streets, and one thing I know to be true; you have to lose your identity if you want to survive the trauma of giving yourself away bit by bit. You have to take on another persona to become a fantasy and play a role in it; you can't do that when your real name keeps reminding you of who you were supposed to be.

You have to lose your identity if you want to survive the trauma of giving yourself away bit by bit.

...

You need to become someone else completely, someone no one has known. It's a way of feeling like anything you do will be your secret, and you can change roles as soon as you change names. I created new names for new towns or different types of clubs that I worked in. I had long ago changed my name when I started dancing to stay as far away from "Kate, the pure little girl" as possible, because I had grown so much contempt for the real me—the one who needed love, affection, and care. I had become so hardened. I needed to be strong to survive, gain courage, and be in control, so I took on names that meant boldness and danger.

I wanted so much to make it in the music industry and in film or TV. I dreamed of becoming a "triple threat" (singer, dancer, actor), but that dream came to feel far away from that young girl; however, I never completely lost hope on her behalf. Meanwhile, it felt like I was trying to outrun something all the time to get to "something more," but it was like being on a wheel, never stopping. Before I knew it, the weeks were suddenly years. I didn't think it would be so long. But now I know it's what they meant when they told a newcomer, "LA will eat you alive." Now I know it means devouring your dreams and innocence.

"Jesse" became my stage name at the first topless bar I danced in. Jesse means "troublemaker with pretty eyes."

I loved Teena Marie, a formidable, white R&B singer known as the "Ivory Queen of Soul." I hoped at some point that I would have the chance to run into her in a studio session or get to audition for her as a backup singer. I felt a kinship with her, so occasionally, I'd use "Teena" as my stage name.

I had different names depending on the type of club and clientele. I also used the stage name "Kori," which I later learned means "a complex mathematical equation that can't be calculated by the human mind." This pretty much summed up the life I had now—Complex.

I tried hard to keep my two identities separate—Kate vs. Kori, my real self and my false self. I stopped using my real name, Kate, only weeks after arriving in LA. No one in LA knew her. Whoever the real Kate was, the one whose name meant «pure,» she was long gone. I couldn't stand to hear my name; it reminded me of my mother's anger. And as for the meaning of my name, that wasn't me; I could never be pure again. It was just easier to forget who I had been or who I was supposed to be. Every time you take on another name, another club, another client, another role, you become more fragmented. It would be a little more than a decade before I would even hear my real name again, and about three decades before I would begin to relearn who that name belonged to.

My real identity was never taken from me. It was just locked up. I locked her away because the real me couldn't show up here, dream here. That was too dangerous. I had learned in my past that any "desire" I had was dangerous and always followed by some form of punishment. Over time my self-contempt grew, and so did the wall around me. It would be a long journey back to reclaim my real name. Finding out who you really are is much harder than creating who you think you need to be for someone else. For now, it was just easier to become whatever a paying customer needed me to be and just get it over with.

QUESTIONS: WHAT'S YOUR NAME?

We are not only given actual names at birth, but we are also labeled with names by family and society that stick with us--such as "disappointment, problem child, dangerous, troublemaker, broken, damaged, fast, hoe, prostitute."

1. What are some of the names you've been given?

2. Which ones have you chosen for yourself (or agreed with) to replace your real name?

3. What do you think of your birth name? What does it mean?

CHAPTER 4

PRETTY YOUNG THING (FLASHBACK)

"What is it about you southern girls?
You can't make the right decisions until
you've tried all the wrong ones."

• • •

remember the first time I got up the courage to go on stage and dance in front of an audience. I was working as a cosmetologist in Atlanta. I spent my days in the salon and my nights partying in the clubs, going to work the next day sometimes without ever going home. Nothing was more of a tell-tale sign that I had been out all night than leaning over to shampoo a customer and having confetti fall out of my hair. The night never started until 10 pm, and we typically didn't get home until around 6 or 7 am. One club had a glass floor with crocodiles underneath the dance floor. I loved a good time and never wanted it to end.

One night I heard about a club that was having a legs contest. The prize was $500. Many clubs had contests, like wet T-shirt contests, to bring in more business. I would never ever do that. I felt I had too much dignity; but a legs contest, although out of my comfort zone, didn't seem like crossing a moral line. I needed to pay rent so that factored in, and I decided to enter it. This was my first experience being in a bikini bar. When I walked in, the bouncer greeted me and pointed me to the bartender, who sent someone to escort me to the dressing room. He asked me what song I was going to dance to so he could tell the DJ. Seeing the stage and lights and dressing room with all the costumes was exciting.

I chose a blue, satin, spaghetti strap minidress that was the same color as my eyes and hugged my figure. About one hundred contestants showed up to enter, but only about 50 were chosen by applause. The club was packed with men, and they called us all out to line up and one by one, do a walk around the stage (to music) and by applause; the best round of applause chose those who would enter the dance contest. Many of the contestants that weren't chosen stayed out in the audience to drink and watch the contest.

Waiting backstage, I was so nervous, but I knew I had to face this. I needed to overcome my fear of being on stage if I wanted to pursue a career in music. The desire to be all I could be in the face of all my fears was at war, but I wanted to overcome my fear and rise boldly to what was being required of me. Each girl had to go on stage alone and dance. If the DJ liked a girl and the crowd was not responding very much, he would comment about her to get the crowd to yell more. But he would end the song short if a girl was too intimidated and didn't dance well. I felt sick to my stomach. What if no one likes me and he cuts my song short? I remembered back to the days of watching American Bandstand and the Dancers on Soul Train and thought of how the best entertainers seemed to melt into the sound. That's what I wanted to do. Just dance. I waited in the wings, watching the other dancers before me and studying the crowd. When it was my turn, I felt like I would faint. I was shaking.

I chose "Michael Jackson's" song, *Pretty Young Thing.* The crowd was settling down from the last girl's performance, and I heard the DJ introduce me.

Suddenly, the music began. I took a deep breath and decided to block out the crowd and listen to the beat. I knew all the words, so I just listened to Michael's voice singing and imagined being in the video. I blocked everyone in the room and allowed myself to melt into the music. I was a natural entertainer and loved performing on stage. It felt like a freeing space to let the little girl who had watched Soul Train finally go for it—dance, sing, and smile. Shrouded in the music, it felt like a safe place to be free and escape everything. It was safe as long as there was a distance between them and me, as long as I was untouchable.

When my song ended, the loud cheers brought me back to reality. I felt like I was waking up from a trance. I began to shake again as soon as I came out of it. I couldn't believe it—I had made it through, and they were cheering and throwing money! When all the dancers had finished, we all came out and lined up on the stage. When the DJ called our names, he'd play a second of our song, and we had to walk to the beat letting everyone look at us again. The crowd would choose the winner; whichever girl got the most applause would win. This part felt scarier to me than dancing to the song the first time. I couldn't lose myself in the song and dissolve from the moment; I had to stay present. Walking out there in front of everyone without the ability to transcend into the music felt so vulnerable and "exposed." That was my biggest fear—feeling exposed! *If they see how intimidated I really am.* The problem is when the music stops, and I open my eyes,

I feel caught and embarrassed for being seen. When someone gets a glimpse of the real, free you, those are moments when you've been caught, and it's literally stunning.

Ultimately, the applause went up when I walked the stage again, and I took home $300 for second place. Even though I felt timid and insecure on the outside, there was a natural entertainer that had just become even more alive inside of me, and I had gotten a taste of what it felt like. I loved the feeling of it; it felt like where I was most at home, and I wanted more. I paid my rent, but I wasn't making enough for the next month and was drowning my depression in partying. I knew it was time to leave Atlanta. I decided to head back to North Carolina to reunite with some of my old beauty school friends.

Like Jake in "Sweet Home, Alabama," said, *"What is it about you southern girls? You can't make the right decisions until you've tried all the wrong ones."* Yep, that was the theme of my life. Moving back to North Carolina was the first in a string of many wrong decisions to come.

QUESTIONS: "PRETTY YOUNG THING"

In this chapter I share a flashback of dancing for the first time in public. It was the first time I felt alive.

1. Have you ever made a decision to step out of your comfort zone that was both exciting and terrifying at the same time?

2. How did you feel afterward?

CHAPTER 5

JEZZABELLE

"In the dark your eyes may adjust, but
it's still hard to find your way out."

. . .

continued to dance at the bikini bar. The money was fast, but it wasn't nearly enough to cover my gas, food, rent, and drug habit, which had increased since I had arrived in LA. I needed more and more drugs to help drown my painful reality. The humiliation and shame were almost unbearable. This was not who I was nor how I imagined my life would be.

Shame says, "I am bad," which felt very true for me, like it had been spoken over me and settled into my core very early in my life, rooted in my conscience. I had heard that my whole life. Whenever my mother was angry or disappointed with me, she would tell me how "awful" I was.

Grief for all that was lost—although I couldn't name it as that—was getting darker, and I was falling deeper and deeper. Like quicksand pulling me down, the more I struggled, the harder it was to move. I finally surrendered and decided to embrace it. I was scared and found myself praying every day for the courage to face what was ahead. It had come to this; I had to betray myself in order to survive. It became more work to hold onto the dream and the hope of the little girl. With each club, music set list, and dollar tucked into my G-string, I had to harden my heart and brace myself more.

The war was between my dreams and my survival.

The war was between my dreams and my survival.

...

That little girl who sang using the hairbrush for a microphone and dreamed of going to California, who collected lightening bugs, took barefoot walks in the rain, and danced as if she was on Soul Train—she was getting harder to remember. This was not the place for her; no place for innocence or hope. She could not come any further with me. I had to forget her, lock her away. Maybe one day, it would be safe enough, and I could allow her to join me again.

For now, I had to find a different way to get through it.

Other dancers told me how they worked at many bars, including a few topless bars where the money was better. They said those clubs were higher end, the girls were prettier, the cover charge was higher, and the customers spent more—if you could get an audition. Some girls got turned away. They would say they weren't hiring.

The clientele was better because they knew the management was picky about who they hired, and so they were prepared to pay more for private dances and tipping.

I did NOT want to go topless! I was petrified of doing this. It was hard enough being in a bikini in front of all those disgusting guys coming in after work, all dirty and smelly. I always tried to act like I wasn't bothered by their stares and comments. In truth, I HATED it. I felt unsafe and afraid ALL the time. I needed to get out of this dive. If the girls said the topless bars were higher class and more money, I told myself it was temporary and would help me get settled sooner so I could focus on my real goal. I decided that to make more; I would have to go to the next level to get ahead faster.

It took me a while to get up the nerve and go to an audition. I picked out my music and went on stage. I had a cute figure and was in good shape. That wasn't the issue. My boundary was being chipped away, and the price was getting higher and higher.

I watched every dancer before me go through a dancer checklist: check the hair, check the lipstick, check the G-string front and back, walk through the curtain and smile, listen to the music and feel the rhythm; watch your balance on this slick, body-oiled stage; be aware of your step, concentrate on what you're doing; grab the pole at the right level; make sure you're in position so your hands don't slip and break an ankle in these 6-inch stilettos and humiliate yourself.

I did my best for the audition, but I was nervous and knew it must have shown. I didn't belong here. I went to the dressing room to change and get my bag of costumes. I expected to be told they didn't need me. Instead, the club owner asked, "When can you start?" They put me into their rotation right away. At first, I knew my sets weren't that good; sometimes, I would even forget to take off my top altogether. Because I loved to dance and escape in the music, before I realized it my second song was ending, and I had totally forgotten to strip. I enjoyed the music so much that a DJ nicknamed me "Little

Timekeeper." For keeping the beat so much that others got swept up in it too. This proved to me that some people were turned on and entertained without the nudity. Nonetheless, it was a topless bar, and I was expected to bare myself. I learned the art of strip teasing as time went on; I was able to take off my top at the last minute without seeming so inhibited and insecure. It's not that I ever felt more secure; I just learned how to disassociate and leave my body when it was time to strip and still stay in sync with the music.

I had moved in with two of the girls I worked with. Both of my new roommates were practicing magic, and they introduced me to it.

We were regulars at the Psychic Eye, a store that caters to the occult. I started studying spells and seeking more knowledge from the books. I began to see things in the spirit world. Literally, the more I was drawn to it, the more access it had to me.

When we all moved in together, we began to dream up a plan to form an all-girl singing group. I suggested the name Jezzabelle. And because I am from the South, belle was spelled with e-l-l-e for southern belle. We got someone to do a photo shoot of us goofing around. We really didn't have a plan for what we wanted. But not long after putting together our group, the other two began to fight a lot, so three became two. We decided to do another photoshoot with the two of us. This photographer was a professional with a studio, which was more of an investment because it cost us more money. This time I knew what I wanted. I told the photographer I wanted a mysterious photo of us coming out of a spaceship door (I think women are from Venus), so he built a set for us. It was a huge side of a spaceship with a round door.

Before the shoot that night, we were getting high, doing some rituals we often did, and chanting the name Jezzabelle. We went to the shoot the next day, and I felt so uncomfortable; something was off.

I had been looking forward to this, but now that we were doing it, I felt uncomfortable in my skin. My roommate, on the other hand, loved it and got into it. We were standing in the smoke, which looked like we had just landed, and we were exiting our ship. It was very cool. When we got the photos back, I was shocked! In the picture above our heads in the smoke was the image of a woman's face. It was just from the neck up, but you could tell she was beautiful, and she was throwing her head back and laughing. I couldn't believe it. I knew immediately it was the image of Jezebel.

After that, we used the photo of Jezzabelle and arranged to be "feature dancers" at a nude club in Arizona. Typically, you were only invited to be a feature dancer if you had some prior publicity, like appearing in Playboy or Hustler magazine (which I had danced at a Hustler event) or some other form of work like porn. No doubt we had gotten the job because of our promotions for Jezzabelle. I knew the money would be good.

We drove to Arizona and checked into our hotel in time to get high and relax before getting ready for the club. We wanted to show up a little late to make a grander entrance; that's what features do, show up later in the night after the DJ has gotten everyone hyped for us to show. In our hotel room, we were burning sage, and she was working some spell over us, calling on Jezebel to come. We had been drinking, smoking pot, and snorting coke because we knew the club was dry (all-nude clubs are). We decided to sneak in our own alcohol at the club. I was just feeling good and ready to be "on." When we got to the club, the energy was great! Customers were already propositioning us, and we were prepared to be the show. The other dancers, however, were rude and hated we were messing with their money, their regulars. I remember "feature dancers" coming to a club I worked in and feeling the same way. Just the title "Special Feature" increases the amount customers are willing to pay for a dance.

Our feature dance together was to "Fire" by the Ohio Players', with smoke machines and lighting effects that were only used for the special features.

After we did a set together, one of the other dancers (the boss's girl) snitched on us about bringing alcohol into the dressing room, and we got fired on the spot. I was in the middle of a private dance when the bouncer came to get me. We went to the hotel, got all our crap, and decided to drive back to California that night, even though it was the middle of the night and we were so wasted. But once we started coming down, my roommate started going off like it was all my fault, screaming and cursing at me; suddenly, she kicked the windshield of my Z-28 with her spiked heel boot, shattering one side completely. I pulled over immediately and said, "Get the f%&# out of my car, b$%&#"! And I drove off with a broken, smashed windshield leaving her standing in a parking lot somewhere in AZ. When I got back to our apartment, I packed up and moved out. I didn't have a plan or anywhere to go yet, so I decided to move around every few days, in and out of luxury hotels, where I could have room service and cleaning service every day. I never saw her again.

Later, I burned the Jezzabelle photos thinking this was the right thing to do.

QUESTIONS: JEZZABELLE

Creating Jezzabelle started out as one thing and ended up being much darker. I ignored my gut and just kept walking forward in the dark.

1.   What does going "too far" mean to you?

2.   Did you have instincts telling you not to?

3.   What was the strong "pull" that made you ignore what you were feeling?

4.   What did it personally "cost" you this time?

CHAPTER 6

IN THE PROCESS (FLASHBACK)

"There was this wonderful-looking creature
with huge hair, a black catsuit, and more
black eye shadow than a drag queen would
wear! Believe me; it was fabulous!"

...

remember back to the day I joined my first band as a lead singer. I was back in NC and had spent many evenings in the recording studio working with other friends who were producing songs and singing back up, while working by day at Profiles Salon owned by JT, a well-dressed white man famous for doing weaves. His entire clientele were Black women and they loved him! By day, JT was a classy salon owner, and by night, he was the infamous Marilyn Rivers, a drag queen and local performing star.

I was always picky about the salons I worked in. After all, I knew the reputation and extent of my training, and not just any salon would do. When I applied to work at Profiles, I was so excited to get in. JT was one of my favorite people, partly because he was funny and dramatic about everything. I loved to hear him tell his version of the story of my first day at work:

> *"I will never forget the day Kate applied for a job in my salon. Now, you have to know my salon was an array of, let's say, different 'types' of people. I had one that was becoming transgender and one who was already complete; my receptionist looked like Diana Ross. This young girl comes in a plaid skirt, white blouse, and navy sweater. As I eloquently put it, she looked like a 'little Catholic girl.' I saw she had talent and hired her. The next day I came in, and there was this wonderful-looking creature with huge hair, a black catsuit, and more black eye shadow than a drag queen would wear! Believe me; it was fabulous! I looked at Debbie (Diana Ross) and said, "Who is that?" to which Debbie replied, "You hired her yesterday." Thank God she fit right in; the friendship has continued for over 40 years. We are all the better for having known Katiedid!"*

One day, JT was doing a weave on one of his clients. Our chairs were right next to each other, so we could talk and join in each other's conversations. He had a client that morning whose name was Paula, and she was talking about her boyfriend, Martin, who had a band. Paula and Martin would be on the road for gigs for a weekend and up to a month before taking a break. The lead singer had just quit, and they were stuck because they were booked for the following weekend. Hearing about Paula's boyfriend's dilemma, JT piped up, "Kate sings."

"Oh really? Well, you definitely have the *look*," Paula said, looking over at me. "Can you sing?" JT blurted out again enthusiastically, "Yes, she can!"

I don't recall him ever actually hearing me sing before, but it was great to have someone cheering for me. Paula asked if I wanted to try out, and I quickly said yes.

JT turned to me. "All right, girrrrl! I got you your dream; now you better promise to come back to work in between gigs!" I loved working with JT, and I hated to leave him, but this was my break! JT also wanted me to get away from Z., my boyfriend. JT always had said, "Katiedid, you can do so much better"—especially since that last incident.

Z was also a musician who was on the road a lot. We had been living together and were madly in love. He was so charming that I had chosen being ostracized by my mother for him. Z. was a romantic, and he knew how to charm me. He could always pull me back in. He was a great cook, and his upbringing by all women taught him to be a nurturer and show love by serving. He would draw my bath after work and make wonderful meals. He'd write songs about me, and he was affectionate and loved to spend time together when he was in town. Until I found out I was pregnant. He was always so in love with me and in love with the idea of having a family together someday. Now, we were talking about aborting our child. I was devastated, and I felt so confused and alone. I loved him, but I couldn't handle the idea of having a child and being all on my own, no Z, no family. He drove me to the clinic and waited outside.

When I got home from having the abortion, I was so weak and in a lot of pain. I laid in bed and cried. Z was very quiet as he packed to go on the road the next day. I begged him not to leave me in this state. My crying and pleading with him turned into a fight, and while we were fighting, the phone rang. It was the lead singer from his band, and she was sobbing too. He left the bedroom and took the call in the next room, closing the door to console her in private. When he returned to the bedroom, he said she needed to talk to him because she was upset; she was pregnant. When I asked if it was his child, he denied it and said they were just close friends. I knew it was bullshit. Everything in my body told me he was lying and that she was carrying the half-sibling of my aborted child. I had suspected he was cheating on me for a while.

I laid in bed the rest of the night, regretting my decision to abort, imagining what it could have been with just a baby and me. In that moment, I hated him! Maybe I *could* have done it alone without him. But now it was too late. I cried myself to sleep. The next day, he left town to go on the road with the band and his pregnant lead singer. While he was gone, I packed everything that was mine and moved out. Many months later, he came crying for me to take him back. He had denied having been with anyone but me, and I wanted to believe the best about him.

One late afternoon, Z and I were enjoying our time off work, hanging out and making dinner together, when there was a knock on our door. It was a sheriff, and he asked to see me outside. I stepped out, leaving the door cracked, and he asked me who Z was to me. "He's my boyfriend," I said. "We live here together."

The sheriff went on to tell me that he patrolled the area, and there had been many nights in the past month that Z had been out in the parking lot, in front of our apartment, in a car with another female having sex. He wanted to know if I knew about this. No!

I DIDN'T know! I was furious. Tears welled up. He apologized for telling me like this but thought I should know what was happening. I turned around to look at Z standing at least six feet away, looking pathetic!!

"What?!?!" I turned around.

He hung his head. "Do you want me to leave?

"If you value your life, you'd better leave with this man," I said. The sheriff escorted him out the door and off the premises. That was the end of Z.

That was the last incident, and JT was ready to see me get away from him for good.

This band opportunity was perfect timing!

The keyboardist and leader of the band was Martin; he was Polish. Aside from him, everyone else in the band was Black. There was G, the bass player; Lars, the drummer; Ra, the guitar player; and Martin on keyboards. They were all good musicians. I packed my clothes, and we all got in a van and took off to Pennsylvania to do a show. I was nervous on stage and uncomfortable in my skin, and it showed. Paula probably had regrets right about then. They kept me on, and I became more comfortable with every set. After a few gigs, I did have to quit the salon. We went on the road so often that I couldn't keep a clientele. Sometimes we would have a weeklong gig, and just before that job was over, we'd get a call from another nightclub in town booking us for another week. So, it was unpredictable how long we would be out on the road before a break in the schedule. I was finally doing what I had been waiting for. And I hoped that my dad was watching me from heaven and was proud.

Initially, I loved traveling and staying in new places all the time. It was like an ongoing party from town to town. G, Ra, and I were pretty tight and liked to have a good time. Our biggest challenge was getting a hook-up with some weed in a strange town where we didn't know anyone. Whenever we traveled, we would arrive just a few hours before the show, set up the stage, lighting, and sound, and by the time we were done with our sound check, we usually had scored weed from some local.

One time we were on stage, G was singing lead on "Word Up" by Cameo.

The guys were having fun getting so into it. I was front and center stage singing back up and watching the crowd, who was also getting into it. The whole room was stoned, dancing, and watching G sing and play his bass. Suddenly I noticed a few people pointing at him. I looked over and saw smoke! G's hair was right under a stage light and just about to catch fire! He was so into it impressing the crowd with his Larry Blackman impression, feeling good about himself; he didn't notice me on the down low trying to get his attention. The band will keep the song going longer when the crowd gets into it because people have so much fun dancing. G kept playing the bridge, over and over, and more and more smoke was coming off his head! I was beginning to panic. Finally, when the song ended, the crowd went wild. Everyone was cheering so loud G thought it was for *him,* but they were cheering because he made it to the end without catching on fire. We had so much fun that night, laughing at G and telling him how hot he was. "G, you were smokin'!"

After our shows, a few of us would return to one of our rooms, have some drinks, and get high. One night when we were in Chicago, I was tired of doing the same thing we had done every night. Tonight was our last night, and I wanted to go out to a party or do something fun after work, but we still needed a car. Uber wasn't a thing yet, and it was late. We always played till 2 am, so nothing was open. The van we traveled in was Martin's, so that wasn't an option; plus, even if we did get him to go out with us, Paula would have his balls in a vice through the phone the next day. That night a group of guys, about seven or so, came into the club where we were playing. They were having fun dancing and buying drinks for the band. We sat at their table in between our breaks while the DJ took over for the crowd. One of them asked us if we wanted to go to a party after the show. G and I both said yes; it sounded like a good way to finish our time there. Ra, however, hesitated. We had to get up early in the morning to load up, and we were leaving for DC the next day.

We tried to talk him into it, saying we would go for a little while. Ra convinced G not to go. I was so disappointed with them for changing their minds. By now, I was already drunk, and there was no stopping me. The guys told us we didn't have to stay long, and after they heard G and Ra telling me not to go, they began assuring me I would be safe at the party with them; it would be fun, and they'd bring me back as soon as I wanted to leave so that I could get ready for the next day.

"I'm going with or without you!" I told G and Ra. G and I were seeing each other, and we had had a fight earlier. I was determined to show him he wasn't all there was.

When our show was over, I got in the car with the guys and left. I don't remember the ride over, but when we got to the apartment, I expected to walk into a full-blown party with people sitting around smoking and having fun. It wasn't uncommon back home. But I became concerned when one guy pulled keys out to unlock the door instead of knocking. When he opened the door there was no one else there—

It was not the party they had sold me on going with them.

They said others were on the way there, and they started pouring tequila shots and passing joints, which I realized after I hit it that it had been laced with something. I got so high; I was standing in the kitchen trying not to pass out when someone put a drink in my hand and then pushed me up against the wall with his body.

I tried to push back, but he pushed back harder and forced his hand up my skirt. I was trying to move and push his hand away all at the same time, but several other guys started circling in around behind him, closing in on me and encouraging him to "do it."

I started yelling, "Get off of me!" But the others were so close in I couldn't move. I was trapped. I was screaming so loud one of the guys stepped forward and said, "okay, okay", then he spoke to everyone else in Spanish, I couldn't make out what he said, but a few of them moved. Then he pushed the main guy off of me, who was still forcing me up against the wall. Then he said, "It's okay; I'll take you back." He grabbed my arm and pulled me out of the circle. When we got outside the apartment, I was so relieved and said thank you so much.

As we started to drive, he was silent. I began sobering up a little from the adrenaline rush and said I was grateful he got me out of there. I noticed we got on the freeway. But I hadn't realized before that we had driven so far away from the hotel to get to the "party." I questioned if this was the way back to the hotel. He said yes, I am taking you back. I said something about how I couldn't believe what assholes his friends were, and suddenly, he reached over and put his hand up on my thigh near my crotch. I pushed it off fast, and in a split second, he grabbed my hair and pulled me over to his side of the car with one hand while driving with the other. I was screaming at him to let me go, and he just kept saying "shut up b*$#&, or I will kill you! He was pulling on me and grabbing with such force he ripped my skirt almost entirely in two and tore one sleeve off my top. I hit him in the face and bit his arm, which had pinned me to my seat. Suddenly, he pulled out a gun and pointed it in my face.

Right then, I had a flashback of my mother telling me whenever you're afraid, call on the name of Jesus, and he will save you. Without thinking, I screamed, "LET ME GO! Then I said, "JESUS!" with authority.

Suddenly he pulled over on the side of the freeway, reached over me, opened my door, and kicked me out while the car was still moving. I hit the pavement rolling, and he screeched off. Worried he might turn around and come after me, I crawled up the hill and got to my feet; I ran into a ditch to hide. Muddy and bleeding, I tried to think, but I couldn't think straight. I did not know what I was going to do. Why did he stop suddenly? I wondered if a huge angel had appeared in that car when I called on Jesus. What else would have caused him to make such a sudden change? Thank God he kept going!

I stood up and crawled out of the ditch. Several headlights blinded me as they passed, but no one stopped to help me. I was in a state of shock and hysteria, bleeding, and my clothes were ripped off. I was trying to hold them together. I started running away from the freeway up a slight hill into the woods. Suddenly, the loud hissing of a semi's air brakes scared me, and I turned to see what was happening. A big, red Mack truck had seen me and pulled over on the shoulder. The driver opened the passenger door and yelled, "Hey, are you okay? Get in!"

I stared at him for what seemed like a long time. My body was in pain, and I was bleeding. I felt paralyzed by fear and painfully aware of the hits and scratches all over me.

"I can help you," he yelled. "Get in!" No way was I falling for this a third time. "No, thanks, I'll walk." I was shaking from the pain of the blows and how I had just escaped death. My head was in so much pain it felt like he was still pulling my hair. "I promise I will get you to safety," he said. "If you don't want to get in, I'll radio the police, and you can sit here in the truck and wait."

I didn't know what to do. I couldn't go to the police. What would I tell them? "I was doing drugs with the guys, and that's why I got hurt," and "I don't know where I'm staying." I couldn't think clearly, so I just kept walking in the dark on the side of the freeway as he rode beside me, trying to get information from me. All I knew was the name of the hotel where we were staying, but in Chicago, there were several hotels with the same name but in different parts of the city. Was it on the east side or west side? I needed to know, but I didn't have a clue. I told the driver I wasn't sure where I was staying. Finally, I decided I had no choice; we were in the middle of nowhere. It was pitch black, no city lights close by or any sign of an exit that might have some form of life in walking distance, much less a pay phone around. I climbed up into the cab of the truck and held on to the door tightly. "Tell me the hotel name," he said. I got out as much as I could before I burst into tears. Fortunately, it sounded like something he could figure out if he was telling the truth.

"I think I know," he said. There are two hotels under this name. "We'll try them both." He drove to the first one, and it didn't look familiar to me, so we left and got back on the road until we arrived at another. This was it! I was back! He got me back safely. I opened the door to get out and heard him say something about being "careful with my life." I said thanks, closed the door, and then turned to see his face once more, but he had vanished. The whole truck! GONE!

There was no sign of anything. No taillights moving down the road. Complete darkness. NO WAY! This is impossible! I stood out in front of the hotel staring into the dark at 5:30 am, wondering what had just happened. I walked through the door of the hotel lobby. The band's lead singer, who had been performing all week, was now bloody and bruised with ratty hair, ripped clothes hanging off me, and smeared make-up running down my face from crying.

The next day, it all felt like a nightmare, except the bruises and pain I was feeling said it was not. I thought about the truck driver and got chills. I wondered if I had been with an angel. I believed in them, I just had never seen one. But I definitely had been saved, and there was no other explanation. I joined my bandmates in the club to break down all the equipment and help pack the truck. I was so sore and barely moving. No one said anything about the bruises and scratches on my body. They knew the night had not ended well for me and could tell it was no time for the usual banter or making jokes like we always did. G had gotten an offer to record with some guys in DC, and he asked me to leave the band and go with him there. I thought it might be better to stay with him. I felt safe with him, and I didn't want to be in the band without him. The rest of the band headed back to North Carolina, and G and I made our way to the producer's home in DC, which had a big studio built onto the house. They seemed surprised to see me with G but treated me decently enough. They offered me a seat and something to drink. I was anxious to hear their material and hopeful they would have something for me in the future as well. We listened to some of the music they were working on, and then they said they'd be in touch with him. G and I spent the next hours searching the city for weed and checking into a cheap motel on the bad side of town. I quickly began to realize that I may have made a bad choice by staying behind with G. It was obvious the producers didn't want me to be part of their plan for him. After staying up all night getting high, I became paranoid about the area of town we were in. We were used to living out of hotels but nothing this bad. And at the rate we were spending money to get high, we'd never be able to afford a real place. We'd be out of cash and on the street soon.

That night I finally fell asleep and got a few hours in before we had to check out. When I woke up, I said goodbye to G. I wished I didn't have to leave. We had chemistry together and shared some great experiences. It was nice to have someone who believed in my dreams, and we had a lot of laughs together in those late-night hours with the rest of the band. G had taught me how to play "Mony, Mony" on bass, and I even played it on stage a couple of times. I felt sad knowing we were at the end of "us," but it was time to move on. I didn't know where to go yet, but even though I was scared, I was determined to move closer to my dreams.

QUESTIONS: IN THE PROCESS

In this chapter, I leave my career of being a hairdresser to pursue being the lead singer in a band, traveling on the road. I was excited to be doing what I loved and wanted to have fun. I always had a deep hope people were good and trusted easily. I barely escaped alive.

1. Have you ever been afraid for your life?

2. How did you escape it?

CHAPTER 7

FRAGMENTED

"The hair on the back of my neck stood
up. I felt sick. I wasn't on my turf, on-stage
where I know the rules of the game."

. . .

Even though I was making decent money working at several clubs in LA, I never forgot about the dream of being a *real* entertainer. I kept my eye on ads in the LA Castings Call for auditions for "extras" for films. If you got a call back to be an extra and could manage a speaking part, then you were eligible to apply for a SAG (Screen Actors Guild) card, which was the goal. Everyone who was anyone had a SAG card. This was the ticket to getting an agent and bigger auditions, not to mention more money.

I was looking forward to that day's audition. Unlike other auditions I had been to that were held at night in old warehouses, this one was in a professional high-rise in downtown LA in the daytime. I circled the block looking for parking, my adrenaline increasing by the minute. Finally, I saw an open spot on the street. I parked the car and sat for a few minutes to gain my composure. As intimidated as

I felt, I hoped I would have what it took to make it in this business. One day I'll meet the right person, get the right audition, and get my big break. Maybe today's that day—the day I'll be *chosen*, I thought. That's what the whole industry was about, being chosen.

I checked my hair and face one last time. Pep talk, "OK, have confidence! I'm 22 years old, 5'5", 119 pounds, blonde, and blue-eyed. I can sing, dance, and act."

But then, so does everyone else in LA.

It takes a lot of courage to psych yourself up for an audition in Hollywood. You're not just judged for your talent; that has little to do with it. You have to be ready to compete against the most beautiful women from all over the world, who come here for the same thing, and some have more courage and drive to get what they want. I had worked in the club the night before and just got off around 3 am. I had to wake up early (meaning during daylight) to make the audition.

Finding the right thing to wear this morning had taken me forever. I didn't have "normal" clothes. All my clothes were exotic costumes. I was creative and good at making things. I made all kinds of outfits for the stage, everything from sheer Egyptian gowns that wrapped around the body with deep "V" necks and front slits, accessorized with handmade jeweled breastplates and headpieces, to Arabic costumes for a "dance of the seven veils," cop costumes, stilettos, and thigh high boots, a dress made entirely from bubble wrap, leather chaps, and corsets with dog collars. I created a gold bikini to wear with a matching dress made entirely out of gold chain, which I specifically made to wear when I danced to Aretha Franklin's "Chain of Fools"— my clever way of coming on stage while sending out a subliminal message to men, which I am pretty sure most didn't get. Smiling at me as I take their money, too stupid to see they are "the fools."

Outside of work, I spent my time around creative people. Many of my friends in the entertainment business (actors and musicians) were indigenous, and being a jewelry designer, I was fortunate to be invited by them to learn their traditions and jewelry-making skills. One friend taught me how to make authentic Ojibwe jewelry.

Another friend was Hopi, and they taught me how to carve kachina dolls. Which I made beautifully, shockingly, and I gave back to him as a gift. I was honored to be invited into some sacred spaces, and practicing these skills became therapeutic and a way to escape to another place. Another very dear friend, Nathaniel, an angel sent to watch over me for a while (a talented blues musician who played bass and sang lead for too many bands to name) and that I stayed with for a while, taught me many things about the indigenous ways of his ancestors and often talked to me about my true calling, reminding me God was watching over me. He showed me how to make a Navajo breastplate out of bone and turquoise that we got from a mine in Arizona. That was a gift, and I will always feel honored to have been blessed by their lives intertwining with mine and for sharing their culture and traditions with me. I will always treasure those memories. (And will teach my son when he's interested, but I'm getting ahead of myself.)

The breastplate I made was displayed in a leather store in N. Hollywood, and later I was told it was purchased by someone who worked with Janet Jackson for a music video. I couldn't verify if this was true, but my piece was beautiful and looked very authentic. I could see that happening.

I had collected some rare stones (from another client who was a lapidary) and made chokers, and sold them to the dancers and other clients in the club for hundreds of dollars. Then I started to get a reputation as a costume designer and jewelry designer among the girls as well. I made a beautiful choker from a petrified cow pie and sold it for $200. That's how I spent the nights I could get all to myself—making, carving, sewing, and designing.

My closet was pretty interesting, to say the least, and I had no clue what normal people wore to auditions, but I'm sure it wasn't something I had in *my* closet. I had shorts and flip flops, and tube tops; that is what I wore *to* work. I wore costumes *at* work, and other than that, I owned expensive, funky, form-fitting evening clothes for clubbing and going to parties and red-carpet events.

My closet mocked me. No matter what I wore to this audition, there was no way to hide who I had become. I longed to find something more than what was there—I longed to be someone else. But being me was a role I no longer knew how to play. My life was about nighttime entertainment. I worked in multiple strip clubs, was a hired escort from 2 pm to 4 am, and designed costumes and jewelry. That had become my life.

> I worked in multiple strip clubs, was a hired escort from 2 pm to 4 am, and designed costumes and jewelry. That had become my life.

...

As I approached the audition building, I wondered if I would be rejected or chosen for this part. Are they watching me through the window and have already decided I'm insufficient? Not pretty enough, skinny enough, tall enough? Is my bone structure strong enough, are my boobs big enough, and so on? I caught a reflection of myself as I walked through the front door. I had to give in to the lifestyle I was leading, and my clothes reflected this.

I opened the outside doors of the building and walked down the hall. Some of the doors were unmarked and I had no idea what was happening behind them. Finally, I saw the suite number I was looking for. I cracked the door open and saw two men seated on either side of a desk. The room was plain and cold. The peach paint on the walls looked dirty under the fluorescent lighting. A lone poster from a film I hadn't seen hung on the wall. Other than that, it was just a desk. Two chairs, a phone, a notebook, and a sheet of paper with a list of names crossed off. The two men turned to look at me. I could feel they were undressing me with their eyes. That's not what I was expecting. The hair on the back of my neck stood up. I felt sick.

I wasn't on my turf, on stage, where I know the rules of the game. I could work a room full of hundreds of men and have them eating out of my hand if I wanted to, but not here in this room... the face they saw was very different from the one that was looking at them. I was neither on stage nor was this a client—a job to get in, get paid, and get out. I was showing up as me and not a persona; I was caught off guard and didn't yet know what was expected.

The playing field was not level. It was definitely to their advantage. The man behind the desk told me I was auditioning for a love scene, and they would need to see how I would do it. I assumed the other guy was an actor, hoping that meant there was a script to work from with him. I wondered if I would have to kiss him. I hoped not, though I knew that was sometimes required as part of the audition. I was willing to do it if I had to for the part. I felt nervous thinking about this. It'd be awkward to do a kissing scene in such an intimate setting.

Both men stood up, and the guy behind the desk moved his chair around to the front of the desk. The other guy slid his chair out of the way. Then he told me to take all my clothes off. What? In shock at the request, I felt paralyzed and lightheaded. It was as if I left my body. I wanted to disappear. I wished I could muster up the same courage it took to get there and look those two assholes in the eye and say, "F%&# you!" and walk out with my pride. But I reasoned this is somewhat normal in auditioning for a part, and that is what I was there for—an audition.

I undressed. I didn't want to look like a prude because I was shaking and scared, so I silently told myself, *don't ask any questions; it'll be over soon.*

Just a few hours ago, I had been looking for the right thing to *wear*. I had felt so hopeful. *Be brave*, I said to myself. Just step out and take a chance. This is what you came for. I tried to convince myself that the right audition would lead somewhere, and then I could do more than just be an extra in a movie. Eventually I would be able to walk away from the nightlife, and then maybe I would have a respectable job to finally write home about.

But at that moment, I was in a room with two strangers staring at me as I stood before them naked. The guy who was standing laid down on the floor while the other one pulled up a chair to watch. I was instructed to sit on top of him. I closed my eyes to avoid making eye contact as I sat naked on top of this stranger.

The man in the chair told me where to touch him and how to move my body.

I told myself I had learned how to play this game in certain settings if I was going to survive; it had made me harden at times, but in this industry, you better know the art of seduction. The trick is making love "when his heart's on fire" ("Hold On," by EnVouge). Even when I hated myself and my heart was hurting, I could fake it and fool anyone. But this was different; this was sheer degradation. This was different because I wasn't hired for this, there was no discussion previously about what I would agree to do or not do. There was just an ultimatum: if I wanted to get into acting, I'd comply.

I could feel the denim and winced as he rubbed against my thighs and pelvis. I could feel evil breathing on my neck. I tried hard to hide my pain. Even in the club, there are rules of engagement between the client with clothes on and the naked dancer. But these rules were not the same. Hope is what gave me the courage to get up and plan to go to this "audition," even though I was totally scared of rejection. It was intimidating to go to anything in this town. Your odds were about 1 in 2 million! That's how many beautiful people you had to beat; that's how many talents you had to be better than; that's how many people you must out-charm. Just to believe in yourself enough to show up and preform, for any casting call or any audition, took some serious determination and big courage!

Hope is what got me out of bed that morning only to be met with degradation and shamed by these two oily bastards!

When I was told I could get up and get dressed, I opened my eyes. The one beneath me was smiling and massaging himself through his clothes, trying to push his erection down. The one in the chair had a wicked grin that made me shiver as he watched me dress. They both thanked me for coming and said they had more auditions still to do and would be in touch. I wanted to wait outside and stop any girl I saw approaching and warn her not to go in, but I felt sick and needed to run. *I needed to run like hell and get out of this town.*

Why didn't I run out of there? I couldn't make sense of it then, but I was in a state of "fawn," a trauma response in which a person reverts to people-pleasing to diffuse conflict and reestablish a sense of safety.

All I could think of right then was getting home to shower! WHAT THE HELL! Why couldn't I get a real break? More and more my hope was beginning to erode. I walked as fast as I could without obviously running back to my car and cried the whole way home. Is this all there was?

Why couldn't I get a real break?

...

Another trap. Another betrayal. I hated myself for having hope. What a fool I was.

I recalled the phrase people say to Hollywood newcomers: "LA will eat you alive." And it's true. Like a million other girls, hope had led me to here. LA has a way of brainwashing every young, starry-eyed girl to keep trying, keep searching for that big break, believing that tomorrow is another chance, and you might make it. Until one day you wake up and realize your dream has become a nightmare. Your dreams have been eaten alive. I became at war with my desire. Even it had betrayed me.

QUESTIONS: FRAGMENTED

This is the story of going to an "audition" for a modeling job only to discover it was really an audition for a porn film.

1. What line/part in this chapter most stood out to you?

2. What does that bring up for you?

CHAPTER 8
FINDING "FAME"

"I heard a voice behind me. *'Are you having a good
time?'* I turned around and recognized him right
away... This was where I wanted to be, what I had
longed to be a part of my whole life!"

...

Eventually I started to find auditions through a casting agency
to be an "extra" in films filmed at Paramount and Universal.
The money wasn't great, but every little bit helped, and being
on the set as a part of a film crew brought me closer to my dream.
This was what I had come for.

One night after working in the club, I convinced my manager
to let me leave a little early so I could go to a casting party I had been
invited to. I remember standing in the corner and looking around the
room at how many people were there. We had all come to Hollywood
from somewhere else, all wanting the same thing—to be seen as
unique and to become a star. I heard a voice behind me. "Are you
having a good time?" I turned around and recognized him right away.

It was Jesse from the original movie *Fame*. He was so handsome! "Yes," I answered. "I'm just watching people." He was taller than me and had dark hair with dark eyes. He seemed to be friends with everyone. People kept coming up to him to say hi in between each question he asked me.

"Are you an actor?" he asked.

"No, I was invited because I was an extra on a film. I'm a singer and a dancer." He was excited when I said dancer and asked if I wanted to sit down somewhere to talk. I said yes in my calmest voice, but in my head, I was screaming, OH MY GOSH!

He was super friendly, a real person, and not at all pretentious like many others I had met. He was curious about my story, so I told him about my dreams and all that had happened to me since arriving (minus the parts about being sold for cocaine by a friend, someone I trusted, and having survival sex to avoid becoming homeless and being pimped out by someone I thought was a boyfriend).

I told him I was working as an exotic dancer in clubs while attending auditions until something better came along. I heard myself say, "I'm just doing this until I get my break."

Jesse became a friend after that night, and we started hanging out occasionally. We went to dinner and a few parties, and he introduced me to other actors. He was always polite and treated me with respect. He was friends with Nia Peeples (also from Fame), an actress-singer-songwriter-dancer who was now the host of "The Party Machine," which was being filmed at Paramount Studios. They had been on *Fame* together and were longtime friends.

"The Party Machine" was like a modern-day "Soul Train," with artists and dancers who got paid to be on the show. It came on Friday night after "The Arsenio Hall" show, so the time slot was great. Jesse offered to help get me on the show as a dancer. The next day, I went to the studio, and my name was on the list. I was buzzed onto the Paramount lot!

It was amazing! Just like in the Hollywood movies I had grown up watching, people were scurrying all around, giant set props were being moved on trucks, and costumes were hanging on racks being rolled to another set. It was marvelous! This was where I wanted to be, what I had longed to be a part of my whole life! I danced for several of the final episodes of The Party Machine before the show was canceled. Getting a paycheck from Paramount Studios felt like a dream come true. Maybe I would make it in Hollywood after all!

Getting a paycheck from
Paramount Studios felt like
a dream come true. Maybe I would
make it in Hollywood after all!

• • •

QUESTIONS: FINDING "FAME"

In this chapter I meet Jesse from the movie "Fame." He treats me differently and gets me a job on the dance show "The Party Machine."

1. Name something you have wanted or dreamed of for a long time that you eventually got to experience?

2. How did it feel to experience a long-awaited dream?

CHAPTER 9

SOUL TRAIN
(FLASHBACK)

"The Hippest Trip In America"

· · ·

When I was around eight years old, my mother started dropping me off at my grandmother's every Saturday because there was no one else to watch me. Mother had taken a job at a children's boutique. It was hard to make ends meet for her. She only got a small Social Security check for us to live on.

It was so boring at my grandmother's house all alone. It was only fun when all my cousins were there for the family holidays. There were no other children around in her neighborhood, so I would have to find ways to entertain myself.

My grandmother loved flowers and birds. She had a big front yard full of bright azaleas and lantana and a manicured backyard with big trees surrounding it. In the center of the yard was a birdbath under a tall faucet with a constant drip to keep it full. In the far back of her yard was a sunken rose garden with a long, raised path running through it. I loved the fragrance of all the roses and the beauty of all the colors. You could often find me playing in the birdbath or hanging out in the roses.

Beyond the rose garden was a small entrance into a dirt alleyway. Sometimes I would go back there after the rain and make mud pies in the puddles of water and dirt. But when she found me out there, I would get in so much trouble for getting dirty and being out of the yard.

Grandmother was a tall, red-headed, fiery Irish woman. She was full of strong opinions and superstitions. She was strict, and being on her bad side didn't take much. The running joke was that everyone in the family was stubborn because of that Mobley "gene" that we got from her. She also had a habit of giving out nicknames if she needed you but couldn't think of your name on the spot. All girls were Sally if she couldn't remember someone's name. she'd yell, "Sal-ehh," raising her voice two octaves on the second half, and whoever was nearest would respond, "Yes, Ma'am?" We'd all laugh because we knew it didn't matter; we were all Sally! Grandmother was known as a GREAT cook! Her recipes were even in the newspaper occasionally. The holidays were always large family reunions. She would assign jobs to all the women to assist her in the kitchen. My three aunts were also great cooks, so she assigned them the main jobs in the kitchen while the rest would get the kids rounded up and make sure the men knew that their time with the football game was about to be put on hold. Everyone would hurry to the table when she called "time to eat." Going to Grandmama's table was something you thought about for days ahead of time!

Men and their rivalry over college football yelling at the TV, women in the kitchen laughing and telling stories while cooking, and kids outside playing games and getting into mischief were what you could count on at a Southern family reunion. I remember one piece of furniture in her kitchen that everyone wanted to sit on—the old yellow stool. It perfectly matched the yellow paint on the walls. It had steps underneath that folded out so you could sit on it or use it for a step ladder. I loved to sit on it and watch everything happening in the kitchen. I learned some of Grandmama's best-kept secrets and best recipes sitting on that yellow stool. My favorite was her famous coconut cake! She would have to make it days in advance and let it sit untouched in the refrigerator. Whenever someone opened the fridge, someone would say, "Don't touch the cake!" But that didn't stop us from asking anyway. "Please, can I have just a small piece?" The answer was always a resounding multitude of voices shouting in unison, "NO!!" My cousin and I would sneak into the kitchen for a homemade treat or a half stick of gum (that's all she allowed) from the gum drawer. We would fight to see who got to sit on the yellow stool and watch the grand finale preparations of the big meal, but of course, once we were discovered, we would get chased out. That stool served many purposes. You could sit and watch Grandmama cook and learn her secrets (and she had a lot). She used it to stand on the steps so she could reach up high to the cabinet that no one else was allowed to get into. There were special ingredients in that cabinet she called "spirits," which were off-limits to everyone else. She used rum for making that special Southern dessert called "Shaaah-let" (Charlotte), and she also kept the blackberry wine up there, which she claimed was only for medicinal purposes when she had a stomachache which, curiously, she seemed to get a lot of when I was around.

But on those Saturdays when I was alone with her, at noon, right after Grandmother had finished lunch, she would always take her nap. She would send me to the den to "nap" while she was having hers.

I would go into the den, close the door, and quietly pull up a stool to sit right in front of the TV so I could be close and it wouldn't be loud.

Saturdays were when my two favorite shows came on back-to-back: the Fat Albert cartoon and Soul Train. I LOVED these two shows, and her nap time lined up perfectly for me to watch the TV.

Fat Albert had a great intro that you had to sing along with, "Na na na—we gonna have a good time." Fat Albert would say his famous line, "HEY HEY HEY." It was a cartoon about a friend gang (not a violent gang) that lived in Harlem, and it always had a life lesson, and I loved all the characters. "Mush Mouth" was my favorite; he was the funny one. "Rudy" was the cutest, and "Albert" was always the kindest. I loved spending time with these characters, and I wanted to be part of their gang.

After Fat Albert came Soul Train. I could not wait for the commercials to end and would get so excited when I would hear the intro – (announcer), "THE SOULLLL TRAAAINN" – and then the opening with the train dancing and coming down the tracks. I'd start dancing right away! I wanted to dance right along with everyone else. Just the opening song would make you move! Then you would hear that famous deep voice from the announcer saying, "Soul Train, The hippest trip in America. We're here with the Soul Train dancers. And I'm Don Cornelius!"

I LOVED to dance! I was always getting in trouble for it, too. The people on the show were alive and free to express themselves. I got to see the bands that made the songs I loved to sing. The only way I could see them was on TV, and Soul Train was where everyone wanted to perform. The Spinners, Tower of Power, Rolls Royce, The Pointer Sisters, The Jackson Five, KC and the Sunshine Band, and those Soul Train dancers! I wanted to grow up and be on that show! I loved the fashion of the '70s, the hairstyles, the clothes, and the music. Everything was so cool, and everyone was so funky and hip. I wanted to grow up to be like that.

The music was so exciting. It *made* you dance! You could tell everyone there was having fun and doing what they loved. Just watching them, I could feel their passion for the music coming from the TV right into you. And I wanted more! I wanted to be in a world where people lived that way all the time.

I needed to be a part of it. But if Grandmother woke up and caught me dancing, which she did on more than one occasion, I would get a spanking not to forget. There were only two doors between us; she was in her room, and I was in the den, only a short distance between my happiness and terror. One time she flung open the den door while I was dancing to Soul Train; she laid into me with a strap.

I thought my mom's rages lasted a long time; from the start of her anger about something, whipping me in between my attempts to get away, until the climax of it all, and then she would finally leave me alone, all of which could easily last 15 minutes. But my grandmother's beating was the longest one I have ever had. She did not stop until she had expressed all her anger about mixing with another race.

I remember waiting for my mother to pick me up from Grandmothers, hoping she would say something to her mother for that kind of lashing. When I told my mother about it, all she said was, "Well, you know you not 'posed to watch those shows!" I don't know why I thought she might take my side and make it right.

It seemed like anything that made me come to life was wrong. I can remember driving home from there, staring out the window and daydreaming of a future far away from here where I could be myself. I thought about the people when they were dancing to the music, I just wanted what I saw in their faces. Joy, freedom to express themselves and not be judged for it. And I hated the racism, although I didn't know that word yet. But I definitely knew what it felt like to be in its presence. I wasn't going to be bound to it no matter what.

It seemed like anything that made me come to life was wrong.

…

And for that, it was worth a 15-minute strap and being yelled at.

Crossing the line for the chance to explore freedom would be a trap for me for the rest of my life. I learned early on growing up in the South that there were two opposing messages people lived by. Southern 101: always be hospitable, put others first, and go out of your way to be kind to everyone. At the same time, always stay with your own people—or else. That's how words like "Darlin'" and "Sugar" could ooze out of one side of someone's mouth while racist slurs could come out of the other.

Interracial marriage had been banned throughout all southern states until 1967, but even then, in many states, the ban was still enforced until 1971.[1] I was only 8 years old, but it was already indoc-

1 "Though federal law made interracial marriage legal in 1967 (as a result of the historic Loving v. Virginia decision), state laws forbidding it remained on the books, and sometimes were enforced. In 1971 a Clayton County ordinary refused to issue a license to John Sanford and Betty Byrom until the U.S. Attorney General's office stepped in. That was the end of Georgia's archaic law."
Bo Emerson, "Even when interracial marriage was against Georgia law, mixed-race couples married," The Atlanta Journal-Constitution, April 7, 2021. https://www.ajc.com/life/even-when-interracial-marriage-was-against-georgia-law-mixed-race-couples-married/OMEGBS

trinated into me that I would be ostracized if I crossed over. And for the South, it would be decades before that was tolerated.

In time, I discovered that "dangerous" came in all colors, starting with my own.

I continued to sneak watching Fat Albert and Soul Train week after week, year after year. Even though I knew what was to come if I were caught, it would be worth it to be part of a place where life was so colorful and alive, if only for an hour—one day. Just maybe one day I could have an experience like that.

Now I can say I did. The party machine was the 90s version of Soul Train. My train had finally arrived.

QUESTIONS: SOUL TRAIN

In this flashback, you get a glimpse of my childhood growing up in a (racist) southern home. The highlights of my Saturdays at my grandmother's house were watching the Fat Albert cartoon and dancing while watching Soul Train.

1. When you were young, did you escape and pretend to be somewhere else?

2. Where (or what circumstances, or who) did you most come alive with (what gave you the most happiness) when you were a child? What was it that captured you?

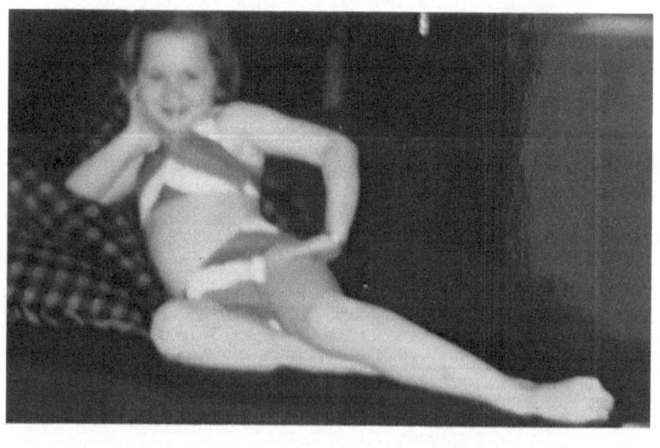

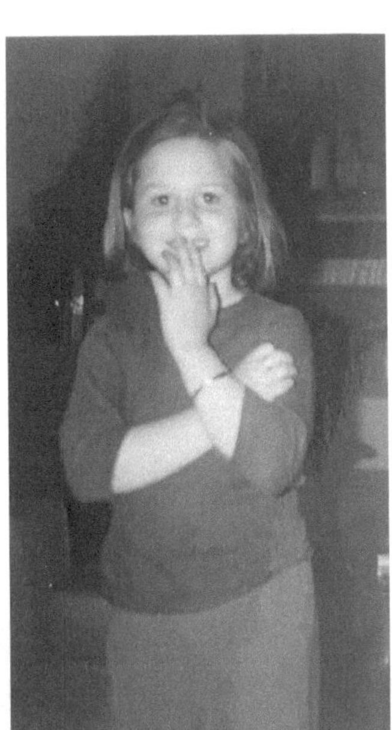
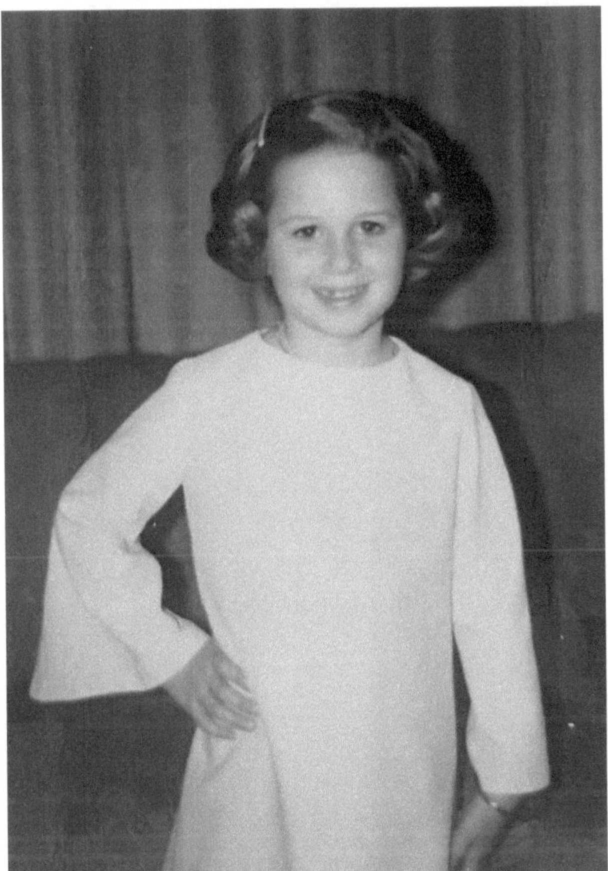

Sebastian cut

Sebastian Artistic center Photo Shoot.

The year I graduat
beauty school.

Androgynous hair photo.

Catlina Island.

Catlina Island,
with a client.

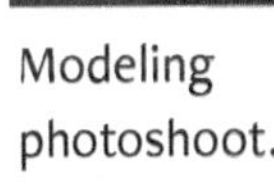

Modeling
photoshoot.

Catlina Island.

Club Audition Photo
(pre-breast augmentation that later
a client would pay for me to get)

Dancers start with D.J. *DOVE*
D.J. Tip Out _DC_ Int.
Floater Dancer count #______ Int.
Bartender Dancer Count #______ Int.
Bartender Tip out ______.

GIVE TO SECURITY TO CHECK OUT.

Club pay out ticket. Dancers had to pay bouncer,
bartender, and house mom before leaving. Dove was
another name I used.

Goldrush Club ID.
Every dancer had to have
one to get in.

Business Card

Jezebelle
first photoshoot.

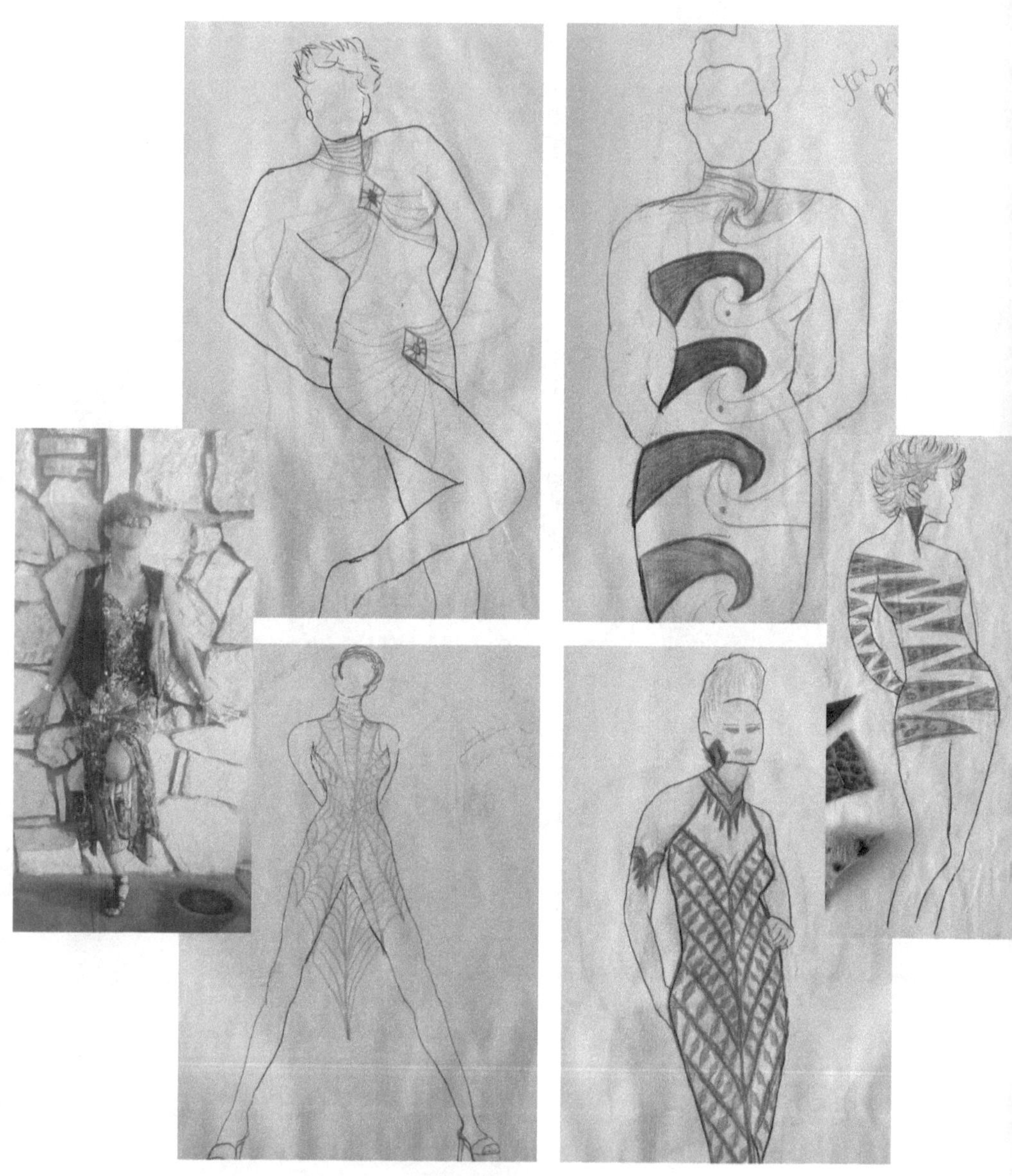

Costume design for stage.

Chain dress.

Leather designs.

Yin-yang deerskin vest I made for one of the dancers.

Native American
Kachina doll.

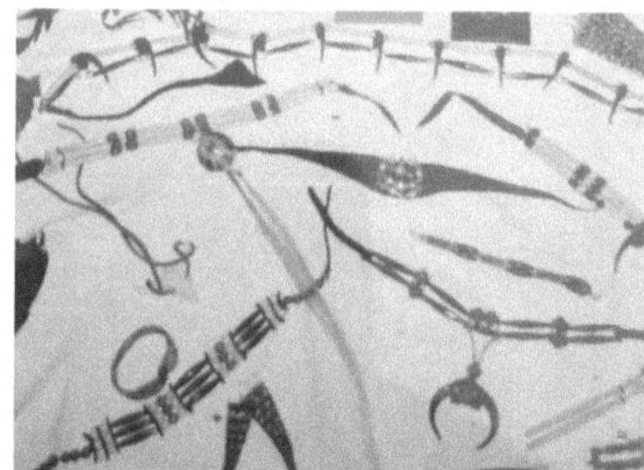

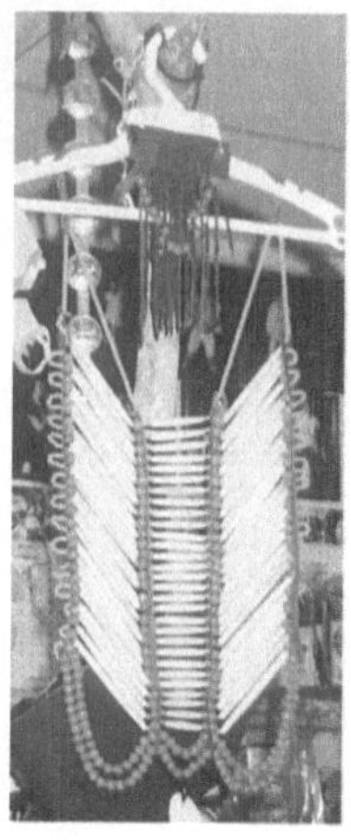

Warrior
breastplate.

Nathaniel Peterson, an amazing blues musician. When I met him his blues band was called Mama Roo, but before that he played with the best in the world, legendary bluesmen such as John Lee Hooker, Howlin' Wolf, Hubert Sumlin, Steve Gaines (Lynyrd Skynyrd), Fred Smith (MC5 guitarist & Patti Smith Band), and Scott Asheton (Iggy Pop's drummer). He recorded with Keith Richards (Rolling Stones), Levon Helm (drummer of The Band), and Eric Clapton on the Grammy-nominated album "About Them Shoes" by Hubert Sumlin, where performed four songs. He also played with the legendary British band Savoy Brown.

The season in my life when he showed up was one of my darkest. I was sure he was an angel who had been sent to watch over me. I still think that. He taught me so much and I am so grateful to have known him! He always pointed me back to the truth. I am happy that before he departed this earth, we were reconnected again briefly. I am grateful he got to see I made it out and was okay now.

I will never forget.

RIP my angel friend. 1952-2023

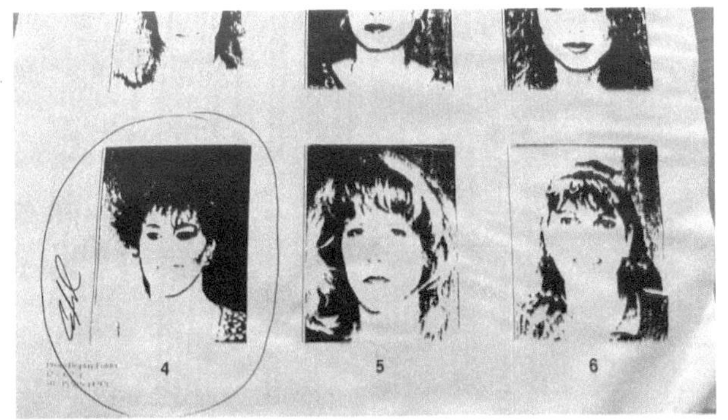

Arrest lineup.

Sybil Brand, women's prison.

Starting Cherished.

We were going to strip clubs for outreach, with our gift bags that had jewelry and lip balm in them. I decided an easier way to get my story into the hands of women was to put a story card in each bag. This is the picture I used on my card, with my story on one side. We put these into the bags, it was quite effective. The women loved opening the bag and reading my story.

Harmony Dust and I in Vegas leading the Treasures (10-year anniversary) strip club outreach. It was the first time I had been back and outreach to the very clubs I had worked in was the only reason I would break my vow and go back to Vegas.

PART 2

CHAPTER 10

DISTORTED MIRRORS

"I looked down at my bare hand. I missed my
ring. I hadn't realized until it was gone how
much it had connected me to my past; it was
the only symbol of any normal life I had had."

. . .

After nearly a decade of working in the commercial sex
industry, I was getting tired and desperately needed time
off. A client I had known for over a year had been asking me
to go away with him for a few days. Although somewhat reluctant,
I finally decided to give in and go to Las Vegas with him. He had made
big promises to show me a good time and give me the break I needed
from all the clubs and clients. He promised no work, just relaxing by
the pool, hanging out together, getting room service in a big hotel
suite, doing some gambling, seeing shows, and just relaxing. Sounded
like just what I needed.

When I met up with him at the Burbank Airport, he didn't have
a ticket for me. He said he hadn't been sure I would be able to go,
so he only had purchased one ticket. We went to the counter and

bought a second ticket in my name. The flight from LA is short. When we arrived in Vegas, he rented a car, and we headed to the Bellagio. He went to the counter at the hotel while I milled around the lobby. When he returned to me, he said our rooms weren't ready yet. The front desk would hold our luggage until the room was ready.

All I wanted was to shower and change my clothes before going out for the evening, but he wanted to go into the casino right away. After about four hours, I started asking if I could go check on the room and relax by myself if he wanted to keep gambling. He kept stalling, and finally, I got upset and said I would go without him. "Let's just go," he snapped at me.

He went to the desk and came back with our luggage. Instead of going to a room in that hotel like he had led me to believe, he had the valet bring the car around.

"Why are we leaving? I thought you said we were staying here," I asked angrily. I was tired, and so far, nothing had happened as he had said. I reminded him of what he had told me. I had trusted him to come in the first place. We argued in front of the hotel for a few minutes, and people started looking at us.

"Ok, ok," he said. "Just get in the car." I wanted to disappear from the humiliation, so I got in the car. Once we started driving, I asked, "Where the hell are you going? You never even planned to stay at this hotel, did you? You lied. OMG! What an ass! You're nothing more than a wanna-be."

He swerved to the side of the road and hit me across the face. "You had better shut up!" he said, clenching his teeth. He pulled back into traffic and drove a little further. We pulled into a sleazy motel parking lot far away from the strip.

"Stay in the car," he ordered, and he went inside to get us a room. Scared and in shock, my shoulders shook, and the tears streamed uncontrollably. He was acting completely different from what I had seen before. A few minutes later, he returned with a key to a room.

The room was dark when we entered it. Cockroaches scampered into hiding as soon as we turned on a light. He shoved me through the door and began to hit me around some more, calling me a b%&#@ and a whore. He made me take off my clothes and get in the bed. For the next three days, he locked me in the room. I was held captive while he abused me. He did whatever he wanted to me, and no one came or asked any questions despite my screams and the noise of him pushing me around. He was up all night doing coke while I tried to sleep and escape him for a few hours. Finally, after not eating for three days, he decided to go out to get food. As soon as he left, I called a friend who was a part of the Hell's Angels and asked for help. He told me to wait there. I hung up the phone and decided I would not wait to see what else might happen, and I escaped through the bathroom window before he returned.

For the next three days, he locked me in the room.

. . .

He had taken all my money from me the minute we got in the room and had thrown away my purse and ID. My suitcase was still in the trunk. All I had to my name were the clothes I had on when we arrived, which were now lying on the floor, and the ring on my finger from my old fiancé Scott, from many years ago when I still lived in

North Carolina. I don't know why I kept it on all these years. It was probably because it reminded me of a time when I had choices and a connection to what seemed like a "normal" past, at least compared to the life I was living now.

I was badly beaten, hurt, and hungry. I had no money and no way to get home. I began running away from the motel in case he returned and started looking for me. I had no idea where I even was. I was crying and running down streets, trying to get as far away from the motel as I could. In that moment, I made a vow, "God, if you help me get out of Vegas, I promise to stay out and never come back!" I was serious!

At about that time, a cab driver pulled over and asked if I needed a ride. He could see I was beaten and had been crying.

"I have to get back to LA, but I've been robbed," I told him.

"Is there anyone in Vegas who can help you?"

I didn't want to call any of the Russian mafia-owned clubs I had worked at before and ask for help. That would just be going from one bad situation into another, and I was in no mental state to work, much less meet their extra demands.

I didn't want to chance running into the client. I knew he'd be at the clubs there, and if I stayed, I would end up seeing him. "All I have is this ring," I said and showed him my hand. "I need money to get back to LA." He suggested I go to a pawn shop. Maybe I could get enough money for the ring to buy a ticket to fly home.

I got in the cab, and he drove me to a pawn shop a few blocks away. I showed the store owner my ring. He could see that I was desperate. He agreed to give me $100 for the ring, just enough to get something to eat and a plane ticket to LA.

The cab driver waited for me while I sold the ring, then drove me to the airport. I was so grateful to him. He even offered to wait around with me for my flight. "You've done so much already. Please don't," I said. In truth, I was paranoid that I would run into the client at the airport. Then what was I going to do? I didn't want to cause any trouble for the cab driver.

When I finally reached the plane, I buckled myself in and looked down at my bare hand. I missed my ring. I hadn't realized until it was gone how much it had connected me to my past. It was the only symbol representing a normal life I had had to hold on to, and now I had sold it to save my broken life. I couldn't believe what I had just been through and that I had gotten out alive. I stared out the window, tears streaming. I repeated my vow, "I'm NEVER coming back," and planned to keep it forever!

QUESTIONS: DISTORTED MIRRORS

Have you ever been trapped in a situation with someone against your will?

1. How did you escape?

2. Vows can be bad like curses, or vows can be good and designed to protect yourself.

3. What is a vow you've made?

4. How has your vow served you?

5. How is it harming you now?

6. Do you need to be released from this vow?

(It's simpler than you think. Listen to Adam Young's podcast on vows on "The Place We Find Ourselves.")

CHAPTER 11

MANGATA

"Looking deep into my eyes, I would stare
at myself in the mirror. Was the real me
even still there; the one who believed that
God was lighting my way by the moon?"

. . .

When I was a child, I used to stare at the moon. I believed that it was following me. ME! I remember walking on the beach at night under a full moon and seeing the silver reflection across the water sparkling like a road on the ocean. That's a Mangata—the reflection of the moon on the water. As I walked, its reflection moved with me. I imagined it was a sign from God telling me His spotlight was on me. That I was special to Him and that He had the moon follow me so that I'd always have light and remember and believe that everything was going to be all right.

My dream was all I had to look forward to. I used to wish that my life would become something special and mean something one day. I even fantasized that I had been adopted, and my birth family was wondering where I was. Maybe they were even distant relations to royalty. I needed a reason explaining why I didn't feel like I fit in anywhere. I needed hope for a future. I dreamed of a family that wanted me and was looking for me. But no one came. I had longed for Hollywood and hoped I'd find fulfillment here. But so far, things were only getting darker, and I felt like I was sinking and there was no bottom. The more I tried to find a way out, the deeper I sank. And no hands were reaching to pull me out.

How many nights had I sat in the dressing room after my sets, staring at myself in the mirror? I dreaded going out on the floor to be groped and degraded by narcissistic men, doing lap dances and talking BS, stroking their fragile egos. Looking at myself in the mirror, staring deep into my eyes, searching. Was the real me still there, the one who believed that God was lighting my way by the moon? Everyone wanted something; everyone was pathetic and lonely. And the worst was that I had become like everyone else—needy, pathetic, and lonely. And I was giving a part of myself away every day to survive. I needed something to get me out of the funk I was in. I needed a purpose, something I could pour myself into that would make me feel like I mattered.

I was giving a part of myself away every day to survive. I needed something to get me out of the funk I was in.

...

I've always had a heart for the underdog, the ones society calls unlovable. I relate to them. LA has a lot of broken people. I gave away so much of the money I earned stripping to people I met on the streets. I could relate to the orphan, and I knew abandonment and loneliness. I remembered a time I had volunteered with the "Big Brothers/Big Sisters" club, an organization that pairs adults with at-risk children to help mentor them. They assigned a little girl for me to spend time with twice a week. She was about seven years old, about the same age I was when I began to feel like something was wrong with me; the same age when my young neighbors sexually assaulted me. She was being raised by a single mother like I had been. I wanted to be there for her and make her feel loved and protected.

During the week, I would visit her house, and we'd color or read a book and talk. We'd go to a park or the zoo on Saturdays and have lunch. She would tell me about being left at home alone a lot. Her house was always messy and smelled of alcohol and stale cigarettes. I dreamed about one day having a huge home and taking all these kids away from these situations so they could have each other and be adopted by families who wanted them.

Honestly, I can't believe anyone ever let me do that for their organization. But this sparked an idea: What if I could incorporate music into helping these kids?

I set out to find a children's home that would be open to having me arrange a concert to raise money to help children who had been abused. I toured a few organizations and said I was considering putting on a fundraiser called "Koncert for Kids." I had no idea what I was doing, but I knew my heart was bleeding, and I needed to make it stop. I thought if I could get an organization to say yes, then I could figure out how to get celebrity talent on board.

I worked in one of the bigger, high-end clubs in LA, where many celebrities came for drinks and dinner. It was common for me to be on stage and suddenly see a familiar face in the crowd—players from the LA Lakers, the LA Kings, actors, stuntmen, recording artists, rappers, music managers, film producers, artists, designers, game show hosts—I've met them all through working in strip clubs. Many club owners were mafia connected and wanted to impress visiting VIPs, so after hours, I even danced and entertained sheiks and princes.

One night I was in between sets. We could go to the bar for dinner if we wanted to take a break. We could bring food to the dressing room to eat or stay "on the floor" and eat, but only if a customer had offered to pay. Then we were allowed to sit with them as a guest. Otherwise, customers couldn't see us sitting around eating or drinking. I rarely ate at work. I was using meth to stay thin and have the energy to work long hours, so I wasn't usually hungry at work. But this night, I decided I would have dinner at the club.

I got dressed for the floor. (We had to wear something interesting but with more coverage than what we'd wear on stage, like a tight dress.) Near the stages were sections (four rows deep) of tables with comfortable chairs (seating for four) to be nearest the stage. Then behind that were bar-like rows facing the stage with seats on one side, the outer tables and booths around the entire perimeter, and in the back, booths with curtains for private dances. I walked past one of the rows of seats on my way to the bar to order something to eat. I looked over to the left and saw my chance to present my "Koncert for Kids" idea to someone who could actually get it done. Sitting at the bar was a legendary, Grammy and MTV award-winning musical artist (in case of legal issues, I'm not disclosing a name), sitting all alone!

I was so nervous but knew I couldn't let this opportunity pass. I *had* to approach him. He looked like he could be a real asshole. I mean, that was his whole gig. I wanted to be sure I had a good segue to talk with him about the concert. I didn't want to approach him like any other stripper who just wanted to make money off of him or sleep with him. I went to the bar and placed my order. I prayed he wouldn't leave yet, or another girl move in and get him to do a lap dance. I certainly wasn't going to do anything like that. Even if he asked, I planned to say I was on break but could talk for a minute while waiting for my dinner. No one had approached him, and he was still alone when I finished ordering, so I took it as a sign that it was my opportunity to go over to him. I walked up and said, "Hi, my name is Kori."

He looked me up and down with that face, no smile. *Don't get intimated. Be confident,* I told myself. I ignored his coldness and continued, "I just wondered if I could ask you a question?" He didn't seem like he was in a good mood, or maybe he was just keeping up his bad boy persona, but I didn't let his non-verbal cues deter me. "I wanted to know if you do smaller charity concerts. I want to do a fundraiser for abused children. I am still looking for an organization to give the funds to, but I wondered if you would help. Would you be interested in being a headliner?" He was quiet for a minute as I waited for his response. Finally, he replied, "Yea, I might. Who's sponsoring it?" At that point, I knew I was out of my league and didn't know how to execute my plan. I told him what I had learned so far. That I was a singer and came to LA for music and we used to cover one of his songs. He made a slight grin at that and told me to call his manager when I had more information. Right then, the bartender called my name. I thanked him, grabbed my food, and headed to the dressing room. I couldn't believe I had just talked to the legend himself, and about the possibility of a collab. For a moment, I wasn't Kori. I was a fellow musician again! I didn't end up following through on the concert fundraiser for abused kids because I didn't know how to, but a seed of hope had been planted in my heart and mind. For the first time, I realized that the experiences in my life could be used for good.

And I would log this idea away for the future and maybe one day...

(To that person) If by chance you are reading this book, well hey, I'm ready to pick that conversation back up, I have a really good charity now and you can sponsor it! PM me ☺

QUESTIONS: MANGATA

At one point when I was in the sex industry, I planned to organize a benefit concert to help orphans. I have seen other survivors do a similar thing. We want to create a home for children so they don't have to experience the pain we have felt of being orphaned. We know what it is like to feel helpless and to have no one come to your rescue.

1. Where do you divert your attention so that you don't have to look at the places where you need care in your own life, where you still need your own healing?

2. When you were younger, what did you dream of for yourself?

3. Have you ever taken a step toward pursuing your dreams? What is stopping you?

CHAPTER 12

MADAM

You must jump into the deep
end—sink or swim, sister!

...

I was in the dressing room with about 40 other girls one night. Some were getting ready for their next set on stage, and others were getting off work and heading home or going out to meet with a client. I overheard two dancers talking about an audition one of them was going to the next day. They looked over at me to include me in the conversation. One dancer told us she was working for a Madam, a woman who ran a high-end escort service in Hollywood. It was through Madam that the dancer met a producer who invited her to audition for a film, and she was so hopeful and excited. I remember hoping for her and imagining with her a new career.

Madam had been a dancer herself. She was a little older than me; I remember thinking "wow, she got out while she was still young and beautiful." She had only recently moved full-time into her role as a businesswoman. (That is the way I saw it then.) She had built quite a reputation, especially among celebrities, for employing only the prettiest girls. The money you could earn working for her was BIG! One job for the Madam could equal more than three shifts at the club unless you had a special "fan" at the club who came just to see you and tipped extra big. Her clients called when they needed an escort for a special red-carpet event, a wrap party, or just for private company. She was extremely selective in who she allowed to work for her. You had to get a recommendation to get an appointment to meet with her before even being approved for an interview. My co-worker suggested I meet her to see if being an escort was something I'd be interested in for extra money. "Who knows," she encouraged me, "You might get your big break through this!"

The Madam agreed to meet with me on my co-worker's recommendation. I debated whether to follow through on a meeting over the next few days. By the end of the week, I had made an appointment and was driving to Manhattan Beach to meet with her. In Hollywood, you quickly learn that with every new person you meet, you must impress them and prove yourself worthy of their time. You must jump into the deep end–sink or swim, sister! But underneath all the attitude and confidence, I felt weighed down constantly by the feeling of not being good enough. I would give myself a pep talk: "This is why you're here, you won't be doing this for long. Soon you'll get your big break." You try to convince yourself you're different, muster up the courage, and get in the car.

The interview consisted of me stripping down so that she could see all of me. "Turn around… yes, you'll be good… you can get dressed now." The following day she called to offer me my first "appointment."

I was not ready for this. I was terrified, but it felt like I had run out of options to avoid homelessness and find a path to getting a break and a change for the next step in my career. The number of people the City of Angels has chewed up and spit out is staggering. The streets are filled with them living under freeways and behind dumpsters. I hadn't come all this way to find my dream, only to give up. I convinced myself that doing calls would be a temporary means to an end. But what looked like a circumstance was a sacrifice to my true identity.

I wondered if I could play the game and meet people who could help me. Who knows, maybe I could charm my way out of having to "do it" at all?

Madam gave me the address and said I'd be attending a small, intimate party. She never disclosed who I was going to meet. I would find out once I got there.

QUESTIONS: MADAM

1. What was a moment when you crossed a boundary because you hoped it would lead to something better?

2. What was the underlying message that you believed about yourself at that time?

CHAPTER 13

FIRST DATE (FLASHBACK)

"On his bike, it was thrilling with the wind
in my face: it felt wild! I loved it!"

. . .

As I drove to the client's house, I found my mind drifting. I thought about the word "date," and how she said, "You have a *date* with a client."

I thought back to my very first date. I was still pretty shy and modest, and I was rather naïve. I was terrified of having sex. I didn't want to go to hell. Raised in a purity culture, essentially, the thought was, "It's your job to keep men from being aroused and looking at you" (misogynistic AND shaming).

So far, my takeaway was that my body was dangerous and couldn't be trusted.

I often felt violated when going to someone's home. It had become just the usual things that people ignored or normalized, like old men making me sit on their laps while they tickled me, causing me to squirm on them. I remember feeling uncomfortable (essentially a lap dance), which I was paid for with candy for the "play." I remember the brothers of my friends bullying, touching, and degrading me.

All of which only added to the shame of developing. I was terrified to give myself away like many of the girls my age had already done. I was taught to believe the fairy tale that someday my prince would come and sweep me off my feet, IF I was good and I kept my virginity! I longed to be chosen and to be safe with my knight in shining armor, and if I were lucky, he'd come sooner rather than later and take me away from all the sadness!

Soon after I turned 16, I went on my first date. I had met an 18-year-old undergraduate student. He was so handsome! When he discovered I only lived 40 minutes away from his college, he got my number and called to ask me out. I was so excited to hear from him! I couldn't believe he liked me. He was so cute with his blonde curls and blue eyes! To think a college boy was interested in *me* felt so electrifying! I dreamed of this and wondered if it could lead to more of a relationship; maybe he was the one I might marry, and this would be the beginning of the future. It took some convincing for my mother to let me go with him to an outdoor concert at his college, let alone ride on the back of his motorcycle, but she finally agreed to let me go.

When I heard his bike pull in the driveway, I ran to the mirror for one last check. My cheeks were flushed with excitement, and my stomach felt full of butterflies. He had driven 45 minutes to come and get me. A few minutes later, we were headed down the freeway and out of town. On his bike, it was thrilling with the wind in my face; it felt wild! I loved it! I didn't know what to say to him while riding together. Thankfully, the bike was loud and hard to hear, so we didn't say much for almost the entire ride back to his campus. I savored the feeling of holding onto him and wrapping my arms around his waist. I had never held onto any guy like this before. When we got to the campus, I noticed trucks parked on the grass where the crowd would have been and the roadies taking down the stage.

I was shocked to see that the event was already over. "I must have gotten the time wrong," he said casually. I was curious about what we would do now that we didn't have a plan. I thought about how far away from home I was and wondered when he'd bring me back.

"Do you want to get something to eat instead?" he asked. But first, he wanted to show me around campus. "Ok," I said as I nodded in agreement; at least he was thinking of something to do. A few students were still milling all around, playing frisbee, lounging in the sun, studying on the grass. College life seemed exciting. For our last stop, he said he wanted to show me the dorms before we left the campus. When we got to his floor, he ushered me into his room. Right away, I noticed only one bed. I thought he said he had a roommate.

Then the door closed behind us. We were on the second floor, so I walked over to the window to look out at the view from the second floor. The leaves were beginning to turn, and for a minute, I imagined what it was like to be away at college, knowing it was probably not in my future. Suddenly I returned to the present when I felt his breath on my neck. "I've been thinking about you a lot," he said as he put both hands on the windowsill, trapping me between his arms. I was glad to hear this, but it surprised me. Of all the beautiful girls, he was thinking of me. I lifted his arm so that I could move to escape, and I excused myself to the restroom to fix my hair from the bike ride.

When I left the bathroom, he was sitting on a giant beanbag chair in the corner of the room. "Come sit beside me," he said. He put his arm around me and turned my face toward his to steal a kiss. My heart was pounding. I wanted him to like me. That was exciting to me, but something wasn't how I thought it would be. I was feeling nervous. I thought we should go somewhere public. We shouldn't be here. It was strange for me to be here in his room, alone. I had never been alone in a bedroom with a guy. My mother forbade anyone but girls to come into my room to hang out. I had friends that were boys in the neighborhood, but they were not allowed into my bedroom; that would go against the sacred purity culture and corrupt my good girl image. I felt like we were breaking a dangerous rule and searched for a way to tell him we needed to leave, but I couldn't think of how to do it and not set off any alarms that made me sound silly. I was worried he would change his mind about me. I don't know how he would react to me, and what if he doesn't want to? Then what? The gravity of being far away from home and unable to get back was becoming heavy. He kissed me again, and I felt his hand slide under my shirt. Reflexively, I pushed him away, and almost involuntarily, I blurted out, "We should get going." He pretended not to hear me and pulled me back tighter, forcing his tongue into my mouth. His kiss wasn't tender anymore, and I couldn't escape him. He pinned me down, my arms with his arms, and his legs forced my legs apart. He pressed down hard on me. I tried to move my head to break the kiss, but he was stronger and kept forcing his tongue into my mouth no matter what I did.

I finally broke free, jumped up, and headed for the door. "We really have to leave NOW," I shouted. I tried to open the door, but it was locked. He came up behind me quickly, grabbed me, and slammed me up against the wall as he unzipped his pants. "You know you feel the same way, and you want it too," he said. I struggled to break free from his grip. I hit him with my free hand, hoping someone would hear the noise coming from his dorm and me yelling at him to "stop," but there was no one around to hear the noise of me falling or being thrown into the walls. He yanked me away from the door and pushed me down onto the bed, sitting on me, pinning my legs down with his. He unzipped his pants and tried to force "it" in my mouth. I turned my face away and tried to break free, but he was stronger than me. In my struggle to get up, my top had ripped open. I was trying so hard to push him off of me, but I was getting weaker after a while; the struggle lasted longer than I could believe, and he seemed to be getting stronger! He pushed me back down and pulled my bra down, exposing my breasts while, at the same time, he finished jacking off. When he was done, he collapsed on the bed beside me. I couldn't believe this was happening; it all felt so surreal. I felt like my body was floating above me and watching the scene. I just wanted to wake up and discover this had only been a nightmare.

Suddenly it shifted from seeing this from above to being in my body again. Every inch of my body was in pain. I felt paralyzed from shock and couldn't move. Then I realized I had to do it, now was the moment I had to get up quickly! I ran to the bathroom and locked the door behind me. Finally, I had gotten away from his grip. My tears burned as they ran down my chapped cheeks, red from his unshaven face rubbing hard against mine. I tried to clean off my body. My heart was racing. He came to the bathroom door, and I jumped so hard if felt like my heart stopped. He tried to get me to open the door. How am I going to get out of this?

Everything in me silently screamed I CAN NOT look into his face again! He begged me to open the door. I cried silently so he wouldn't hear me. He would speak kindly and say he was sorry, then after a few minutes of my not responding he would break the silence by hitting the door, jolting me again! This went on for what seemed like an hour. I couldn't bring myself to open the door. I felt paralyzed. Over and over, he promised to take me home if I would "Just open the door."

I was so afraid of who would be on the other side of the door when I opened it – the guy that was polite and nice or the violent asshole who had just assaulted me. What if I come out, and this time, he rapes me? Deep inside, I was scared, but at the same time, a wave of anger and fierceness was rising in me; I finally got up the courage to open the bathroom door. I vowed to do whatever I needed to protect myself. I opened the door forcefully and walked out. He followed me out of the dorm and down the hall. Neither of us uttered a word. I mentally prepared myself for the possibility that he might try to do something else to me on the ride home.

We got on the bike, but this time, I felt disgusted having to hold onto him. The ride felt long going home, and my body felt weak and bruised. I hoped to get into my house without my mother seeing me or wanting to talk. He looked so pathetic and helpless now. Not at all handsome and strong. When he pulled into my driveway, he asked me again not to tell anyone and said he was sorry. I looked at him with disgust but said nothing. I turned and walked into the house, my skin crawling as I heard him drive away. It felt surreal, except for the pain I was beginning to feel all over. I felt shaky, but I couldn't let my mom see. I told her we had been sitting in the grass at the concert, so my legs were itchy, and I needed a shower. I sat in the shower and cried. No matter how long I was in the shower, I couldn't get his smell off me.

I was devastated and shocked at what had happened. I felt ashamed and stupid for wanting a relationship to develop with him and allowing myself to even dream of it. I wanted to believe someone could want a real relationship with me and that he was good. I had let myself hope and, again, was betrayed and violated. I concluded that there is no natural goodness regarding men, relationships, or sexuality. And if I never wanted to get used against my will again to satisfy someone's lust, I would have to get tough and be in control.

QUESTIONS: FIRST DATE

1. Do you remember the first time you had hoped that someone cared for you and you began to dream of the future?

2. Do you remember the first time you were made to feel afraid of your sexuality?

CHAPTER 14

PILLOW TALK

"It was too late; walking out
would have blacklisted me."

. . .

This was the address. I drove up the steep driveway and parked my car. I took one last drag of my cigarette before putting it out, then a quick, final check in the mirror. I slipped on my heels (I always drove barefoot) and got out of the car, unsure of what to expect. I was nervous and hoped I was dressed appropriately for the occasion. I took a deep breath and rang the doorbell. A man opened the door and welcomed me in. He was older, maybe mid 50s. He had dark, curly hair that was just beginning to gray in places. I noticed he didn't button his shirt up all the way, and you could see some chest hair, a telltale sign he thought he was sexy. I caught a whiff of strong-smelling cologne, expensive, no doubt. As I walked past him, I noticed his jewelry, also telling; he likes to flaunt his money. I would need to watch out, I thought. He might be one of those guys who comes on strong as soon as he's got me cornered and might try to stiff me.

The house was beautiful. This was exactly how I imagined music producers and people in the movie industry lived. As we walked into the living room, you could see all the way through to the back side of the house, which was all glass. The view from the terrace was breathtaking. You could see the city lights that stretched out for miles and miles. He called my attention back to the room and introduced me to a few other people, first names only. I wasn't sure who they were, so I didn't act impressed. Truthfully, I never knew who would be in the room, and it would have been worse to let them know I didn't "know" who was in the room; better to act like I didn't care and just listen and put things together on my own. I sat down on the sofa, and someone passed me a joint and asked If I wanted a glass of wine. "Sure, thank you," I said, relieved. I needed to relax. I wasn't sure what was about to happen. I was in a room full of total strangers who could ask me to do almost anything. I was trapped.

Once you're there, saying "no" isn't an option.

I felt myself unwind as the weed and wine kicked in. The man sat close to me and rubbed my back and legs while conversing with his guests. The night finally began to wind down, leaving me alone with the client. *Here we go*, I thought. I needed to get ready to sweet talk him and then make my exit, which wouldn't be easy. Once we got into bed, we talked a bit about the music industry; the talent he represented was impressive, and there happened to be one I loved who was an icon and really everyone's favorite R&B singer! He asked me why I had come to LA. And I shared a little of my story. I thought he would decide to let me off the hook and maybe offer me a chance to go to an actual audition for the record label. Instead, as soon as there was a pause in our conversation, he was on top of me. It was over as fast as it had begun.

Disappointed that I didn't get to finish my conversation with him about an audition, I got up to use the restroom, hoping I could get dressed and make a quick exit, feeling like I had blown my chance. Just as I was about to get dressed, he asked If I would stay the night. I told him my time was up, and the Madam expected me back. "What if I call her and make new arrangements?" he asked.

The Madam had warned me not to ruin her reputation with any silliness or misconduct. I'd better be classy and always "be agreeable" to keep her customers happy no matter what. I wanted to leave since I knew this night wouldn't amount to anything more than sex. But I was afraid to make my Madam mad, so I complied with his request.

"If that's what you'd like," I answered. I got in the shower to help with my headache while he called her and made the arrangement. As much as I had hoped we were done, I knew this was about his ego. He wanted me to stay so that he could wake me for round two when he could "get it up" again. As soon as daybreak came, I got dressed. I didn't stick around for coffee and small talk the next morning. I collected my money before he could even get dressed.

It was early morning, but I knew I had to drive straight over to Madam's condo to give her the money. She lived in a beautiful condo right on the beach, which one of her clients had "gifted" to her. One entire wall in the living room was a saltwater aquarium full of exotic fish. She had a housekeeper, and someone else came once a week just to take care of the fish. She drove a brand-new sports car and wore beautiful clothes. She knew everyone that was anyone and had all kinds of connections. She reminded me that she didn't get here by being stupid.

When I was tired and didn't want to go to work, she would remind me that this was what I signed up for. I wasn't going to meet these people without her help. I'd better not ruin her reputation; no flaking. Always bring back the money when it's over because she would send someone and get it regardless, and I *would* be blacklisted in the entertainment industry just for knowing who the clientele was. She began to call me often for jobs. Sometimes I would be on my way to a shift at the club, and she'd say, "You must take this, or I'll give it to someone else. You don't want to miss out on this opportunity!" I would have to call in sick to the club and go get ready to go on a date for her.

One night when I was at work, she paged me. I went to the bar and asked to use the phone to call her back. She gave me an address in Hollywood and said to go after I got off from work.

Working for eight hours dancing and then going to a "call" was not like working a second job after being in fast food or retail all day. What appeared empowering and glamorous was mentally and physically traumatizing. Physical stress is hard on your body; being on stage dancing in heels climbing up poles, falling off of the pole onto your back, and being knocked off slippery tables by drunk customers takes a tremendous toll on your body, sometimes up to 16-hour shifts a day. I was changing costumes in a dirty dressing room every 30 minutes. Constantly redoing your hair is damaging, and re-applying full makeup is a lot of work; the smell of cigarettes and alcohol and men's cologne begins to seep into your skin, and you can't get it off, having to be "on" after just being sexually assaulted for the thousandth time and smiling while playing the head games of men trying to sell you any lie they can to get you to fall for it. With each sickening comment, each hungry eye, each terrifying touch, each dollar placed in my G-string while a hand tries to cop a feel for more than my thigh, I had to muster the physical, mental, and emotional resilience to endure these sexual assaults over and over, night after night. Even when they placed the money at my feet, my value and worth were still mocked as I'd lean over to claim my payment off the dirty stage or table.

What appeared empowering and glamorous was mentally and physically traumatizing.

...

Fortunately, on this night, I was working in a high-end club when I got the call about my next appointment from the Madam. This was a "super club" with around 300 girls performing every shift simultaneously on three stages in the main room and another full-size room with ten smaller stages for "shower dances." The shower stage room was a separate room designed with stage lighting, platforms, and its own DJ for music. There were several shower stages in the room, so there might be a few going on at the same time, each with its own stage lighting and their own camera for the customer to get all angles of the dancer he just paid for. There were no curtains like in a lap dance booth. In a shower dance, we were on stage and completely exposed. The cost of a shower dance was more because it involved more eroticism, and frankly, it took up more of our time. They were two songs long instead of one, as was typical for a table dance, and after a shower dance, we'd have to redo our makeup, blow dry, and style our hair to be ready for another set on-stage or to get back on the floor. You had to know how to time it in the rotation to be prepared and back on the main stage by your scheduled time. After the phone call with Madam, I planned. I would do one more set on stage, and then find someone who wanted a shower dance so I could kill two birds with one stone—make more money and be showered and fresh for my date after I got off work. The Madam typically booked me for the week, so I knew most of my main appointments ahead of time. But sometimes, she'd call me for a last-minute appointment. I hated those because I hadn't had time to mentally prepare myself to go. This was one of those nights.

As usual, she didn't tell me who the celebrity client was. I always had to show up, not knowing who I would be meeting. "Cocktail Party" meant I was going to someone's house for a cocktail party and not a public location, like a bar or a restaurant, and to wear something to impress the guest and always wear something sexy underneath for the client for after the party. Sometimes I would meet the client at his house first, and then we'd be driven to a party. I never knew exactly how to dress or what they expected. For this night, I put on a dress. Something I thought would be appropriate to show up in a white form-fitting backless cocktail dress with a plunging sheer "V" in the front. When I pulled up to the house, there was a steep driveway. I had to use the emergency brake to park. *I hope it holds*; I thought as I leaned down to put my stilettos back on. I hoped no one could see me through the large windows struggling to finish getting dressed. I exited my car and walked up the steps to the gate. I could see the house was amazing through the windows.

I rang the doorbell, and a handsome man in his late 40s or early 50s with gray eyes that popped against his tan skin opened the door. Even though his hair was receding to the point he would soon be bald, what remained were salt and pepper soft waves. He casually buttoned the bottom of his shirt when he opened the door but stopped halfway up. He greeted me and invited me in. The house was totally what I imagined living in LA would be like. I had been in a few like this with similar layouts—large windows across the back with a fantastic view of the valley sparkling with lights. There was a large deck off the back and a pool. The reflection of the water shimmering danced on the ceiling, making the mood all the more mysterious. Even the bathrooms had the touch of an interior decorator, accented with beautiful live flower arrangements with tinted colored water to match the flowers.

I followed him into the living room, where he poured a glass of wine for both of us. There were a lot of photos of him with other actors around the room. He said there was a get-together tonight that he'd thought about going to but didn't feel like going out. Would I mind if we just stayed in? I should have convinced him to go to the party. But I didn't know him well enough yet. I could have met other people, made such an impression on everyone there, and then rocked his world. He would put me on speed dial, and I would have gotten that break, cast in a movie I hoped for. But instead, I just settled for doing what I was paid to do. "Yes," I said with a smile. "Let's stay in, just the two of us."

"This way," he said, leading me down the hall and into the bedroom. As I drove away that night, I replayed my pillow talk conversation with the client. I learned he produced some major films. I pretended not to be star-struck. *How could I let that night end without a plan to see him again? To audition for him?* I didn't want to expose myself for who I really was, not this persona I had to pretend to be, hired to do a job. I didn't want to come off like everyone else that met him. I didn't want to come off desperate.

I never wanted my life to be like this, but now that I was in this situation, it was too late; walking out would have blacklisted me.

Damned if I do, damned if I don't! I stewed over my choices. He did call me a few times to "escort" him to a party after the screening of a new film or a jazz club to see a friend play. Once to a Lakers game, right on the second row behind the players (I was not too fond of sports and was so bored), but I liked his company. With him, I could hear about the life I dreamed of, the life I was sacrificing everything for.

QUESTIONS: PILLOW TALK

1. Have you ever wanted have the respect of someone you thought was important?

2. Have you ever wanted to be a part of something but felt like you were on the outside looking in?

CHAPTER 15

GOLD RECORDS

"It's all smoke and mirrors."

...

On another night, the Madam gave me the address of a client in Hollywood. The apartments were beautiful and old and had probably been in Hollywood since the 1930s. I'm sure they have been home to many celebrities over the years. I stood for a minute and imagined probably many had walked through the same garden courtyard I was about to enter. I pressed the number I had written on the paper, and the gate buzzed and opened. Just as I started walking through the courtyard, a man stepped outside his apartment.

"Hi, are you Kori?" he asked in a British accent.

"I am," I answered, trying not to sound nervous.

"Come on in," he motioned. He had shoulder-length, dark, wild, curly hair. He looked like a rocker. He wore jeans and a t-shirt, nothing special, unlike many of the calls I had been to where I'd be greeted by someone who looked like they were expecting a date and had put some effort into preparing for it. I could see he hadn't even picked up the place before I came over. I thought, Ok, that's a bit cocky. Who does this guy think he is? It looked like a rock star's hotel room.

I asked if I could use the restroom and quickly assessed that this was just a crash pad, not a place where he lived permanently. It was small and had the basics—a couch and a coffee table with a pipe and some weed, a small kitchen table with an empty pizza box, and an unmade bed in the bedroom. One used towel was hanging in the bathroom, and there didn't appear to be extras. I was beginning to feel uncomfortable. This was not what I had experienced from the Madam's other clients. I was trying to decide whether to stay or make an excuse and leave. I left the bathroom and looked again at the unmade bed across the small hallway. Who else had been in there, and how long ago? I noticed no art on the walls except for one framed gold album hanging over the dining table. I strolled back to take a closer look at it. Anyone in LA can have a gold record in their house, even if they've just worked in the recording studio where it was recorded. Maybe he played or did sound for someone who got a gold album, or perhaps his studio got the award. I didn't know. I looked closer, expecting to confirm my hypothesis, and then I saw his name and the record. I knew the name, but what band he was famous for being with again wasn't registering.

I shrugged and walked back to the couch where he was sitting. He pretended not to notice I was looking at his trophy on the wall and loaded the pipe. He was probably waiting for the a-ha moment he usually gets when someone recognizes him, for a million questions, or for me to ask for his autograph. I wasn't into rock and roll anymore, I hadn't been since high school, so it just didn't connect.

He asked if I was into music as he took a hit and handed me the pipe. "Yes, I'm a singer. I'm into R&B," I told him. I was probably becoming more disappointing to him by the minute. I was obviously not a rock and roll groupie; I didn't have long, rocker chick hair (not today, anyway). I had shown up in my natural hair (not extensions), which was more of a Hale Berry pixie cut. I wasn't wearing leather pants or a leather jacket like most rockers in LA wore. Instead, I had put on my favorite clubbing outfit, a tight black Norma Kamali hot pants jumper that zipped up the front. It had a tight fit and flare jacket that zipped up the front and flared at the waist. The jacket zipped up on top of the jumper, making it look like I was wearing a super short jacket all by itself. And, of course, stilettos. Always stilettos. He offered me a beer. I wasn't a beer drinker but took it to be polite, and we sat on the sofa smoking the pipe and getting stoned. Really stoned. Which helped kill the awkwardness I had been feeling. He asked if I was from LA, and I told him a little about my journey, leaving my work as a hairdresser to follow my dream of music to go on the road with a band for a while, then coming on my own to Hollywood, and how I was working as an exotic dancer and escort while waiting on my break into the music business. I said "This was temporary," and I planned to stop working in the clubs (and for the Madam) as soon as possible. He told me a few of his "on the road" stories. It didn't feel like a client relationship but just hanging out with a fellow musician like we were at an afterparty talking about the love of music, drugs, and hardships of that lifestyle.

After getting high and having some interesting conversation, it was time to get down to business. I started making out with him on the couch so I wouldn't have to go to that unmade bed. When my time there was over, I was still stoned. It was dark out, just before twilight, when I left. Ultimately, he was just another call, someone I would never see again, and that was all.

The next day, it finally clicked who he was. I had to laugh. Oh my gosh, it's obvious now! A flood of high school memories came rushing back to me; getting stoned and floating on the lake with the music echoing out over the sound; or sitting and starring at their album covers for hours. Who would have guessed I'd end up having an intimate encounter with one of the most legendary guitarists of all time and not even know who he was? That must have been disappointing for him. I felt sad more than star-struck. He was just another client, and as much as I was making a name for myself in elite circles, it wasn't for my singing, acting, or dancing. Meeting famous people wasn't helping me reach my goal of becoming a triple threat. Who was I kidding? I had one role to play: an escort. The industry treats escorting as a glamorous life, but the kind of people who call escorts and what they want from them isn't glamorous. It's all smoke and mirrors. I came to Hollywood hoping to meet the singers, actors, and dancers I had admired from all the old classic movies I had grown up watching. Those were my dance teachers and why I was so good at it. It turns out that getting paid to date the stars helped me see that they're just broken people, too, many with addictions and sick fetishes. Those people had done the same thing I was doing, locking away our authentic selves and real hope. A part of them had died, too, to take on a false persona to "make it." That's the real story behind the fetish, addiction, and need for porn.

As much as I was making a name for
myself in elite circles, it wasn't for
my singing, acting, or dancing.

...

To quote Dan Allender, therapist, author, and speaker, "It's desire gone mad."

In all my years of walking around Hollywood and going to parties, only one person left me feeling star-struck. Not long after I had first arrived there, I had been feeling lonely and underwhelmed living in LA. I was still reeling from all that had happened to land me there. Things were not exactly going as I had planned. To cheer myself up, I got dressed and decided to take myself out to a late lunch, just me all alone.

I drove into Beverly Hills to go sightseeing; there were still so many places, restaurants, and boutique shops I had not been to. I pulled over to an area where there were shops thinking I'd walk around a bit first; shopping always made me feel better. Besides all the shops, another thing I love about LA is the al fresco dining. I love that about CA. The weather and the sunshine feel so good. All you want to do is be outside. While walking and window shopping, I noticed a cute little ivy-covered garden tucked back from the street and realized it was a restaurant. I walked around to the front and decided to go in. It was dimly lit inside and nearly empty. After all, most people eating this time of day had either gotten a late start on their day or were suffering jet lag and probably still on another time zone. The maître d' escorted me to a corner booth, and I moved into the center of it so my back would not be facing the door. I always watch the door. He handed me a menu. I tried to keep a poker face when I saw the prices and realized this wasn't the kind of place you go to alone for lunch. It's where you go for a very special occasion. I wasn't going to leave now and humiliate myself. Plus, I was just as special as anyone else dining there. It had been hard since arriving in LA and so full of disappointments, so I decided I deserved this. I ordered a glass of wine and said I needed a little longer to look at the menu, thinking maybe I'd just order an appetizer and a drink instead of a full lunch. A few minutes later, I heard the waiter taking the order of someone near me; his British accent and the tone of his voice were very distinct, and it caught my attention. I looked up and saw he was talking to Ringo Starr! I couldn't believe it. He was sitting two booths away. Alone. I tried not to stare. I went to the restroom to walk past him to ensure I wasn't imagining anything. It was him, for sure!

As I returned to my table, I passed him and looked slightly up to catch his eye. He looked up at me and nodded and smiled as I passed. I hesitated for a second. Should I? Then he looked down, signaling there wasn't an invitation to make conversation. I kept going and went back to my booth. When the waiter came over, I whispered to my server, "That's Ringo Starr!" He nodded yes and put his fingers over his lips. "Do you think I could get an autograph, maybe?" "No, please don't ask him," the waiter whispered. "He doesn't want to be bothered right now."

I was disappointed but not rude. I respected that he didn't want to be bothered. I knew he had seen that I didn't force the issue, and I decided I'd let my memory of sitting two booths away from Ringo Starr remain a real Hollywood moment for me, the Hollywood I dreamed it would be. The Beatles were huge when I was a kid in the 60s, and after all those years of screaming girls, he still had the same effect. Here we are 30 years later, and he still made the girls scream, and now I was one of them too. I was just screaming quietly.

QUESTIONS: GOLD RECORDS

1. Have you ever thought someone else had the power to "make you" or give you what you wanted?

2. What did it feel like to have your future be at the mercy of someone else?

3. What have you had to do to make yourself go through with "it"?

4. When did you decide not to trust you own gut/instinct?

CHAPTER 16

DUNGEONS

"I felt myself leaving my body..."

• • •

One night the Madam called me late. I had worked at the club, so it was already after 2 am. I was exhausted, and taking her call was the last thing I wanted to do. But if I didn't answer, there'd be hell to pay.

"I've got an appointment for you. This one's special," she said. "It's one of my personal clients, and I want you to go this time. But first, you'll need to stop by my place to pick up some things to bring with you."

When I arrived at her condo, a black leather duffel bag was waiting inside the door. "Here's the address," she said as she pressed a piece of paper into my hand. "And don't forget the bag!"

"What's is this?" I asked, thinking it was something personal that belonged to the client that I was returning. All she said was, "Don't leave anything there. Bring the bag and all its contents back when you drop off the money in the morning."

I went to the car and unzipped the bag. I opened the bag and was met with a thick combination of leather, dark heavy oils, and incense smells. Inside were all kinds of dildos, whips, handcuffs, cock rings, and other toys—some I had never even seen until that moment. For a minute, I thought about returning to her door and saying, "I'm not the one for this client." But I knew the stakes were too high.

When I arrived at the address, only the front porch light was on, which worried me. *What if I go to the wrong door at this hour?* I left the bag in the car for now in case I was at the wrong place. I walked up to the door. It opened before I knocked, and a short, balding man peeked from behind the door, motioning for me to come in. He had been waiting at the door for me to pull up and said he didn't want me to knock at this hour. Feeling completely creeped out and afraid, I went into the dark house and wondered how to escape this. He told me to follow him to the back room of the house. I assumed we were going into his bedroom. But when he opened the door, the room was empty except for three things—a chair in the middle of the room, a cage that would be a tight squeeze for a medium-sized dog, and a blacklight bulb screwed into the overhead light fixture, which I didn't notice until he flipped on the switch. He turned to me and asked, "Did you bring the bag?" He was annoyed that I had to go back to the car to get it. He walked with me all the way to the front door to watch and make sure that no one saw me and that I wasn't bailing. When we finally returned to the room, he told me to strip down, open the bag, and put on the leather pieces. The scents made me feel nauseous. He watched me as I undressed and picked up the thong, the leather harness bra with chains, gloves, and a leather mask that covered my eyes only.

The items were small, and I hadn't noticed them in the bag earlier. I don't know where it came from, but he handed me a tube of dark lipstick and told me to put it on while he watched. Now that the bag had been opened, the smell was growing stronger, filling the room with its heavy, nauseating odor. With a pit in my stomach, I put the lipstick on. He proceeded to explain each piece of equipment and how I should use it. He wanted me to tie him up and told me to be forceful and aggressive, and if I didn't, I would be punished. I knew he'd punish me whether I followed his instructions or not. It was what he had paid for. I had never done anything like this before. It was degrading and disgusting to do what I was required to do to him and with him. I wish I could have just funneled all my hate for men onto him. But instead, I felt myself leaving my body shortly into the session; I don't remember everything that happened.

It was daybreak when I finally left his home. I hoped no one would see me leaving.

How many girls do his neighbors see leaving this house? I wondered if they left feeling the way I did, nauseous and sore.

The twilight made everything seem more surreal. I don't even remember driving home; I seriously wonder how I made it without being pulled over. That happened a lot.

I was driving while completely dissociative and wondering how I made it home the next day. I couldn't wait to get home. I don't know how long I sat in the bathtub.

Underwater I could silence all the sounds that went with the images in my head. It could have been hours. The water had gone cold when I finally got out. And it didn't matter. No matter how long I sat there, I couldn't have washed away the stench of the night. It was still so strong to me. I called the club I was scheduled to work in that night and told them I was sick.

I couldn't eat anything at all. I felt nauseous, although that's not the only reason I couldn't work. There was no way I could dance tonight. Every part of my body was screaming and on fire. I couldn't even recall how each happened as the pain and bruises set in. My skin felt like all my nerves were on the outside and were raw, and I certainly didn't feel like talking to anyone. I didn't want to have to explain the cuts or give anyone any idea that I was "about that" and then get even more propositions from those kinds of clients.

With the bath towel still wrapped around me, I went straight to bed and slept until the next day. For the next few days, I felt like I was walking in the intermedia, and there was a war over my body and soul. But there was nowhere that I belonged.

There was nowhere that I belonged.

...

I hoped I never got called to return to him, but he was just the first to come, and there would be other fetishes to quench.

QUESTIONS: DUNGEONS

1. When did you have to do something that you were disgusted by?

2. How did you feel afterward?

3. Do you ever think about it?

CHAPTER 17

CHILDHOOD GAMES (FLASHBACK)

"A stinky smell I didn't recognize came
from his room. *Maybe it's just the way
a boy's room smells,* I thought."

...

As I drove away, I thought about the first time I walked into something unknown and was forced into something I didn't want to do.

A new family had moved into the neighborhood two doors down from our house. There were two kids, a girl about my age, seven, Sara, and her brother, who was about eleven, Mark. As usual, everyone had congregated to play together in the yard. Sara and Mark must have heard the laughter and came outside to see what was happening. Someone asked them to join in our game, and Mark came over with confidence. Sara moved more timidly, like she needed her brother's approval to join in. But I could tell she was curious to see who we were and what we were doing.

By the clothes they wore, they looked uncared for, or maybe their family didn't have much money. Not that any of us did. We didn't have much money, although my homemade clothes were always clean. Sara and Mark's clothes seemed slightly too big or too little and were often torn and smelled funny. I felt sorry for them and pretended not to notice.

Sara invited me over to their house to play. I didn't want to go there by myself. I hoped I could get Jennifer to go with me, but she wasn't home that day.

We could get some of the other neighbors to play outside, so I wouldn't feel awkward about going into their house alone. But none of the other kids seemed to be around, so there was no one I could ask to go with me. Truth be told, their parents probably would have said no. No one knew much about the new family.

None of my diversion tactics worked, so I asked my mom if I could go to their house, hoping she would say no. Instead, she was glad for me to go somewhere without bugging her, so she said yes. I walked through V's front yard to their house, wishing her car would pull up so she could go with me. I hoped Sara's dad wouldn't be there. Something about him made me feel nervous. I couldn't explain it; I just felt anxious about him.

I was trying to be brave. I walked up to the front porch, took a deep breath, and knocked on the door. No one answered right away. Phew, I thought, maybe they had to run a last-minute errand. I turned to leave, but suddenly, the front door opened. Mark stood in the doorway. A strong smell hit me in the face, a combination of mildew and cigarettes. I pretended not to smell it and tried not to twist my face. I didn't want him to see that I was struck by it and hurt anyone's feelings. Mark pointed to the hallway. "Sara's in her room."

I walked down the hall thinking this house was just like Jennifer's next door, with the same layout. But unlike Jennifer's, I didn't feel excited to be here to play. It felt different—musky and dirty.

Clothes lay in the hall on the floor. Mark's room was off to the left, where Jennifer's room was in her house. A stinky smell I didn't recognize came from his room. *Maybe it's just the way a boy's room smells,* I thought.

I could see Sara's room straight ahead, where the parents' room should be. I went into her room, and she closed the door after me. The room was a mess. I could see an unmade full-size bed under the pile of clothes. Maybe this was her parents' room. Come to think of it, I had never actually seen her mom, only a man, who I assumed was her dad.

The bedroom looked and smelled like it had never been cleaned. Odd since they hadn't even lived there long. On the floor and dresser were dirty dishes with crusted, old food. Potato chip bags and candy wrappers were layered on top of dirty clothes and underwear. My mom would never let me leave my room like this, I thought. She would never even let me out of the house, let alone have someone over, with my room looking this way. I would have gotten beaten with a belt or a hairbrush, whatever she could find for making this kind of mess! Sara already had a game planned for us. "Hey, let's play dress up!"

"Okay," I answered. Saying no didn't feel like an option. I didn't have any other ideas, and dress-up was usually fun. I liked playing dress-up because I loved costumes, but it was hard to tell the dress-up clothes from the rest of the clothes thrown all over the room. Sara looked around and pulled out a blue, slightly sheer nightgown from under a pile of clothes. "Here, put on this dress," she said as she handed it to me. I was confused; this wasn't a costume. Clearly, it belonged to her. I didn't want to embarrass her for not having dress-up clothes, so I played along. Maybe they were too poor to buy Sara costumes, and this was how she played dress-up.

I started to put it on top of my shirt and the shorts. "No!" she said, "You have to take your clothes off, or it won't look right!" I felt uncomfortable, but I didn't know what to say. "Ok," I said hesitantly, "but I want to go change in the bathroom." "You can change here," Sara said. "No one will see you." I was so uncomfortable undressing in front of her, so I said, "I need to use the bathroom anyway," and I took the dress into the bathroom to change. When I came out, Mark was in the room with Sara. "Mark is going to play too," she announced. I wondered what game we were playing that he would play with us. I guessed we were going into the backyard to play a pretend game, and we all had to be in different clothes or something.

Surprisingly, Sara removed her shirt right before Mark and changed into another blue and white see-through nightgown. It looked a little like a dress-up nightgown. Maybe it was the only "pretty" thing she had, and she wanted to pretend it was a fancy dress.

"What are we playing?" I asked. "Let's play house," Mark answered. "I'm the dad, and you're the mom." So I pretended I was cooking dinner, and he acted like he had just come home from work. We make-believed we were a family, and Sara was our little girl. After we ate our pretend supper, Mark said, "It's time to put Sara to bed." We said good night and put her to bed. Then Mark said, "Hey, let's play another game. This time, you can be the mom, and Sara can be the dad."

"What? Why?" I asked, confused. Without hesitation, Sara said, "Okay, yes! It's nighttime, and we're all going to bed now."

"Okay, change clothes," Mark said. "Sara, you can be in your underwear. Both of you get in the covers and go to sleep." Now, I was a little nervous. The gown was pretty, and I could pretend it was a fancy dress in another game, but I didn't want to go to bed with Sara, and I definitely did not want to change in front of Mark. I didn't understand why Sara and I should be the mom and dad and get in the bed under the covers. Sara quickly took off the gown and stood there in her underwear as she tossed the gown into my hands. She pushed the pile of clothes off the bed onto the floor as I was leaving to change in the bathroom again. When I came back into the room, Sara was already in the bed, and Mark was sitting on a chair off to the side.

"It's nighttime, and you have to come to sleep now," Sara said. I walked over and slowly got in the bed, pulled the sheet over me and pretended I was falling asleep.

I wanted this game to end. I was feeling very uncomfortable, but I was afraid to say anything.

"You have to kiss goodnight," Mark said. I looked at him and said, "No, I don't want to do that!"

"It's just pretend," Sara said. "We have to. You're the mom, and I'm the dad."

With enthusiasm, she quickly got on top of me. "Let's fake kiss like this." She put her hand over my mouth and moved her head back and forth, pretending we were kissing like in the movies. It was so strange and felt weird, and I started to get up. "Hey, it's just a game," he said. "You have to kiss too. It's just pretend!" Sara started to pretend again. I squinted my eyes tight; I just wanted it to be over. I didn't want to do it, but I didn't want to say no and make them not like me. Why couldn't my mom call me to come home now? I listened hard, hoping to hear her voice. She always called me home just when I was having fun, but now when I needed someone to get me out of there, no one was there to save me. I was also scared that their dad would come home at any minute, and what would he do? Sara kissed me again the same way, keeping her hand over my mouth. But this time, she pushed her tongue between her fingers, forcing it into my mouth while holding her hand over my lips and pushing her hand into my underwear. She began moving her body in between my legs, pressing her pelvis on mine.

"Roll around back and forth like you are making love," Mark said.

I didn't know what to do. I wanted to run, but I was scared. I noticed that Mark had moved his chair in front of the door. I felt trapped. I knew this was all wrong, and I wanted them to stop playing this game. I suddenly felt like I was watching us from outside the room like I had floated away from myself. Mark stood up and pulled the sheet off of us so he could see everything, and I could hear him breathing hard as he was telling Sara what to do. That's when I saw that his pants were open, and his hands were on his "thing." I had never seen one before. I felt scared and sick all at once. Suddenly I screamed, "No, stop!" and jumped up.

Mark turned and ran out of the room with his hand still in his pants.

"No, don't go," Sara pleaded, pulling her underwear back up.

"It's just a game. We can play something else."

"No, I have to go, or I'll be in trouble. I need to go, or my mom will come looking for me."

I went to the bathroom, changed quickly, and ran out the door, hoping no other neighbors saw me leaving their house. I felt so ashamed and dirty. I was sure my mom would notice and assume that I had done something wrong, so I decided to hide in our side yard near the carport before going into the house. I felt "filthy" (a word I heard from my mother describing me when I was dirty). I sank between the house and a shrub and cried. I never told a soul what had happened that day.[2]

"A study of 200 juvenile and adult street prostitutes documented extremely high levels of sexual child abuse in their background. Sixty percent of the subjects were sexually exploited by an average of two people each, over an average period of 20 months. Two-thirds were sexually abused by father figures. The abuse had extremely negative emotional, physical, and attitudinal impacts. Seventy percent of the women reported that the sexual exploitation definitely affected their decision to become a prostitute. The others reflected the influence in their open-ended comments. Findings make a unique contribution to both the studies of the antecedents to prostitution, and the long-term impacts of sexual child abuse."[3]

OK, before you turn the page or close the book…

I think it's important for you to know right now, if you have experienced anything like this, you may feel like throwing this book across the room. Believe me—been there, done that!

---

2 "Child on Child Sexual Abuse (COCSA) is a form of sexual abuse where both people are minors. There can be more nuanced [sic] in these cases; fifteen-year-olds, while still minors, can consent to sexual activity with each other, but not to adults. Some people define COCSA as before puberty or before a certain age (often between 12 and 14); some jurisdictions' laws also place a necessary age gap between victim and perpetrator. However, any and all people, no matter the ages of perpetrators and victim, can be sexually abusive."
"What Is Childhood Sexual Abuse?," *Survivors Healing Survivors*, Accessed September 8, 2023, https://csasurvivors.home.blog/what-is-childhood-sexual-abuse/

3 Silbert, Mimi H., and Ayala M. Pines. "Sexual child abuse as an antecedent to prostitution." *Child Abuse & Neglect* 5, no. 4 (1981): 407-411.

The shame and anger that comes up over some memories can feel unbearable, and you are thinking if I started opening those wounds, once the tears start, they would not stop and I might fall apart, but it isn't true. You made it this far and now you are ready. You are brave, you have a lot to offer. You are meant for more. You are worthy of getting to the other side of this pain. The shame you've been holding all these years over that memory doesn't belong to you anymore.

I tried to shake the memory and make myself think of the good part of my childhood before they moved in when my neighborhood was still fun and innocent. There was nothing like springtime in the South, especially the smell of honeysuckle and the sight of wisteria blooms in the breeze.

In Georgia, there are a lot of pine trees; when the wind blew through the trees, it sounded like a crowd whispering. Sometimes I would just lay in the grass and listen to those trees.

I remembered the giant old tree in my front yard. It had the most enormous wisteria vine that I've ever seen wrapped around it. The wisteria flowers were huge and had taken over, and you could barely tell the overgrown vine apart from the old tree's trunk.

When the wisteria bloomed, the tree looked like an enormous umbrella of cascading purple flowers. I loved lying under that tree in a bed of purple petals. I wished I was back there right now. I could almost smell those beautiful, intoxicating flowers thinking of it.

The "lyyyyte-nan bugs" (that's how we said it in the South) would come out at dusk to usher in the summer night. My best friend and I loved to capture them in jars and pretend they were our lanterns, setting them beside us as we lay in the grass watching the stars come out.

Jennifer lived next door. She was one year older than me and had an older brother and a younger sister. We played almost every day and did everything together. We were both in love with David Cassidy from *The Partridge Family* TV show, so we'd take turns pretending to be his girlfriend while the other had to settle for his younger half-brother, Shaun.

We would spend hours making up dances and rehearsing them over and over. My house was on the corner of Whispering Pines Road. Another favorite pastime of ours was standing out in the yard, waiting for a car to drive by so we could pose like statues. We thought it was hilarious and believed we were so good at it that some people were probably fooled and thought we were yard statues. We'd laugh so hard we'd practically pee in our pants after a car passed at the thought of how we had fooled them! One of my best memories is of us walking barefoot in the summer rain under our clear umbrellas. We loved to kick off our shoes, grab our umbrellas, and walk for blocks in the warm rain, just kicking through the puddles. We loved walking in the water. The rain would run on the side of the road like a mini river next to the curbs, rushing into the gutters. We could walk for blocks and blocks and be gone for hours. No one ever worried or came looking for us.

Our neighborhood was full of families with kids, all between the ages of six and sixteen. Except for me, I was the only child at home. Almost everyone went to the same schools, and many of us were close in age.

My best friend's yard was the only one without many pine trees, which created ample, open space in their front yard for us to play. This became the gathering place where everyone would meet up after they got home from school and ate a quick snack, then we'd meet for games. Freeze tag, Red Rover, we never ran out of ideas. Jennifer's parents were both teachers and always had fun stuff for us to do. They had a giant parachute, and there were just enough of us to go around it and lift it up in the air, then bring the edges back down and make it into a vast dome. We would all go inside it just at the last moment, laughing and waiting for the dome to collapse so we could do it again. We had so much innocent fun. Rain or shine, back then, kids had to be called in from playing outdoors. No one wanted to be inside and sit in front of a screen. We didn't have video games and movies at our fingertips; you had to go all the way to Sears at the mall to play the simple video game pong. My childhood was all about being outdoors. Like most kids in my neighborhood, my mom liked me playing outside as much as possible. I liked it too.

We'd play all day long until, one by one, we were each called home for supper. But afterward, everyone would meet up in the open lot and play until the bug truck came through to try to wipe out the mosquitos, which are terrible in the South in the summer. The bug trucks would drive up and down each street at dusk and spray a thick, white, toxic cloud into the air. The air was so foggy from the spray you couldn't even see your hands in front of your face. We loved it! If one of the neighborhood kids weren't outside in time, we would run and knock on their door and tell them, "Hurry up, the bug man is coming!" Our game was to run, chasing each other into the plume of spray until we disappeared in the fog. The mosquito spray signaled the grand finale of another summer day.

QUESTIONS: CHILDHOOD GAMES

1. Is there a story or memory that you feel shame over and have even perhaps buried deep and never told anyone?

2. Do you remember a time that should have been innocent but turned into something you did not expect that made you feel dirty?

3. How long have you kept that secret?

4. What would it feel like to be free of the secret?

CHAPTER 18

SYBIL BRAND

"I laid in the street with guns
pointed down at me."

. . .

After being in LA for ten years, I learned my way around this city and a few others, working at every strip club in the circuit: LA, Vegas, Atlanta, Fort Lauderdale, and Arizona. I was making good money, but I typically spent it on drugs. I was doing almost anything, snorting and smoking everything handed to me: coke, meth, PCP, mushrooms, hash, pot, pills, and alcohol. I never wanted to be sober because I didn't want to think about how far away I was from my dreams and who I had become. I was still coerced to work for the Madam if I wanted to "make it." And I was renting a room from a guy I knew was a pervert and who was probably dangerous. He was a drug dealer and had wired the whole house to videotape all activity, including watching me take baths and have sex with my fireman boyfriend when he dropped by to visit.

I knew I wasn't safe living there, but I didn't feel like I had any other options for where to live at that time. If I told anyone, I knew he'd find out. So many times, I wanted to cut the wires I would see running thru my room in the closet, but I was afraid of what he'd do to me when he found out. One day he was working on a friend's car, getting it ready to sell for him. "Why don't you drive this car to work tonight," he offered. "If you like it, you can buy it when you get back."

I was about to work a double shift and knew I could make enough tips from both jobs to pay for the car, so I took him up on his offer. I headed to the topless club first and worked until 1 am. Afterward, I headed to the nude bar for the 2 to 4 am shift. Like other nude bars, this one was open after hours and didn't serve alcohol. Literal busloads of male tourists would arrive. They'd order orange juice, sit directly in front of the stage, lean their heads down low, and look up, trying to see our vaginas. If you asked if they wanted a private lap dance, they'd pretend there was a language barrier and couldn't understand the question, even though they'd tell each other right in front of you what you were asking. Most of them just wanted to pay the cover charge, drink their OJ, and watch the show without tipping. I was grateful when, occasionally, the manager would walk by when I was dancing and tell them, "No tip, no seat," and try to make them move away from the stage so tipping customers could sit there instead. They would all put a single dollar on the stage in front of them so he would leave them alone. Then when you thanked them and picked it up, they would talk to each other shaking their heads in disappointment. It was SO frustrating! I hoped things would pick up when I noticed two famous actors walking through the door. All the dancers noticed them too. These guys were in the prime of their careers and could have been out with any girl in the world, yet here they were at 2 am, walking into a XXX bar.

I was on stage, which was long and practically took up the length of the whole building; there were three dancers on stage at a time.

I kept my gaze on the actors, wondering where they would sit—at the back of the room, at a dark booth, or stand at the bar? When they walked up to the stage and sat right in front of where I was dancing, even though I was excited to see them up close, I was disappointed they were in the club. It just goes to show fame and fortune don't satisfy. Everyone is lonely.

By 4 am, I was exhausted and ready to head home. I smoked a quick joint and left the club still dressed in my "on-the-floor costume." (This was a sexy outfit, like a short-shorts jumper or a short, tight dress, that I'd wear to go out on the floor to talk with customers; in other words, not regular clothes.) As I was driving, I noticed a police car change lanes to get behind me, and it followed me as I turned onto Lankershim Drive. I saw flashing lights in my rearview, so I pulled over. The officer immediately started talking through the bullhorn, telling me to get out of the car and lay face down on the road. I had no idea what I had done that warranted them treating me like a high-threat criminal. Shaking, I got out of the car and stood in the middle of the street. Even at 4:30 am, North Hollywood is a busy area. Cars zoomed past, and I feared I might get run over.

Suddenly, two officers jumped out of their car, pulled out their guns, and pointed them in my direction. Two more police cars pulled up and formed a circle with their cars to surround me. All six officers stood behind their car doors, guns pointed at me.

All six officers stood behind their car doors, guns pointed at me.

...

"Lay down," two officers shouted at me, one repeating what the other said to intensify the situation. I was in shock. I had no idea what was about to happen or why. Once before this incident, I had been arrested after getting pulled over for a traffic violation when the officer discovered I also had a warrant out for my arrest. I had to ride to the police station in his car, but the matter was quickly resolved. This was clearly something much more than a traffic violation. I couldn't understand why this was happening.

I laid face-down on the pavement, guns still aimed at me, while two officers searched my car. They asked where I was coming from and where I was going. "Any drugs in the car?"

I knew better than to lie, so I said yes and told them where they were stashed. They impounded my car, handcuffed me, and put me in the back of the police car without telling me why I was under arrest. I sat silently in the back seat, bewildered and afraid, as we drove to the station. Once there, I was booked for car theft and drug possession. Car theft? What? When I heard that, I thought they were talking about someone else. I thought I was test-driving my roommate's friend's car to decide if I wanted to buy it. That dirty a$#hole had set me up!

I was trying to tell them what he was like and that it was a setup. Of course, no one would listen. They just laughed at me. Meanwhile, the real criminal is at home going through all my s*%&! What a scumbag!

The next thing I knew, I was transported to Sybil Brand, a women's prison. My freedom was gone just like that, and I still didn't understand why. Sybil Brand was a maximum-security facility designed to house 900 women with a peak occupancy of 2,800. This was the infamous prison that once housed Susan Atkins (her confessions to a cellmate at the prison led to the arrest of Charles Manson and family). When I arrived, it was filled to capacity, so until a cell opened, they put everyone in a big room with about 200 other women sleeping in bunk beds, much like a Turkish prison. The guards never knew when you were being beaten up or sexually assaulted because they weren't in the room, and there were so many women in the room it was easy to cover things up. The others would surround the bed so no one could see what was going down. They covered up for each other, and you'd better not snitch!

The shower was the most dangerous and harder to escape. Someone would come into your shower while someone waited outside to keep watch. If you weren't being sexually assaulted, you were having your underwear stolen. The guards would not give you a new pair, so you had to wear your gown without underwear, making you an even easier target. That was the point. I had short blond hair, so right away, one of the old-timers nicknamed me "Blondie" when I first arrived. I didn't get my first phone call until days after I had arrived at Sybil Brand. I called the only person I thought could help, an attorney who also happened to be a client of mine, hopeful that he'd be willing to help me out, especially after all I had done for him. But he was in no hurry to see me in court. "I'll see what I can do," he said. I knew all his bravado was BS. He used to call himself my "Superman," which helped him get it up. OMG, talk about ego! What a coward, afraid to let the cat out of the bag. One word and the judge and his wife would find out how he was a "John."

Time moved so slowly in prison. Every minute reminded me of everything I had done and what my life had been until this moment. Early in the morning, guards would call out the names of those who were due at the courthouse that day, and you'd better not be late!

If you still had some soap, you could shower, then get in line to be handcuffed.

I got on the prisoners' bus early to go from Monterey Park to Valencia to be at the courthouse by 7 am. I arrived at court hoping beyond hope that I'd be released. Instead, when it was my turn, the judge announced an extension on my case and set a new court date. I was crushed. I had prayed so hard that the judge would release me and I wouldn't have to return to Sybil that night. With handcuffs binding my arms, I boarded the bus for the long trek back to the prison. Sadly, this would become a routine experience over the next three months. Each time, I'd go to court, hopeful that this nightmare would end so I could go home. But just like the first time, the judge would push my court date out again. Once his gavel hit, it was written in stone.

The disappointment of hearing my name called to get back on the bus for the long ride back was almost more than I could bear. The powerlessness I could not escape. Life inside Sybil was horrifying. Women were ruthless to each other. Sobering up in prison and being assaulted by other women leaves its own set of Post-Traumatic Stress Disorder impressions.

I didn't eat anything but oranges nearly the whole time. I saw how the women on KP spit in the food if they didn't like someone. They didn't need a reason. If they didn't like your face, you were a target. People were always stealing anything you had, and you could do nothing about it. You just had to live with it. Once, someone stole my underwear when I was in the shower. I had to go days without any until the guard decided to help me out and gave me a new pair. They were way too big, but I couldn't complain.

The girls in the bunk next to me were constantly having sex. Even though they hung a towel over the side of the bunk, I could hear every sound. There was nowhere to go. It's no wonder so many people find faith in prison. You evaluate your life decisions and swear to change whatever you can just to get another chance! I had a Christian upbringing, so I remembered Bible stories and prayed. A LOT! I would try to negotiate with God and remind him of how he had opened the prison doors for Peter (Acts 12: 3-19). Why not for me? (Maybe I got the story wrong and said Paul, and that's why he didn't respond!) At the time, I blamed the attorney for screwing with me and not getting me out sooner. After all, I had been there for him on those late-night calls. I expected him to return the favor.

I hated my time in Sybil, but now, I can see that it was probably exactly what I needed. For one thing, the situation with my drug-dealer roommate was escalating. Who knows what he would have done to me? I do not know what he did with the videotapes he made of me. I might have been the next thing he was going to sell.

The judge ordered me to attend drug diversion classes while I was in Sybil. This gave me a chance to rethink my choices, and for the first time, I was beginning to see the adult entertainment industry for what it really is. I knew one thing: I didn't want to return. But I would be broke and homeless as soon as I was released from prison, and the Madam didn't want anything to do with me now that the police had caught me. I had spent the past decade living in the night, stripping and escorting, I desperately wanted this to end that life, but I didn't know what else to do. I felt trapped.

But how do you make a change when all you can put on your resume is 100 strip clubs you've been in rotation for, for the past ten years? Where do you go when you walk out of jail with a felony on your record and no money to eat with? When the only person offering a hand wants something from you, wants a piece of you…and you have no other way. What do you do?

QUESTIONS: SYBIL BRAND

I couldn't trust my roommate (he set me up and called in the stolen car), and I couldn't trust the cops (they were ready to shoot me), and I couldn't trust the attorney, who had been my client (he was a coward and didn't want to get busted for being a "John.")

1. When have you been so deep in trouble that no one would help you and no one would listen?

2. Have you ever had your freedom taken from you?

3. Have you been made the scapegoat for what someone else did?

PART 3

CHAPTER 19

UNLOCKING THE CAGE

"It was the greatest birthday gift ...the gift
of discovering I'm worth so much more!"

• • •

When I was released from prison, I had no money and no idea where to find a decent job. I wanted to move out of the pervert's crack house. But for now, I knew if I wanted to eat and get back into the house (the neighbor was watching for me) to get my things and my animals (birds and kittens), I needed money, quick money! I owed my housemate a few months' rent from being in jail, and he was the one who set me up and had me arrested for car theft. I couldn't trust him for anything. I'm sure he went through all my personal things while I was away, and I just hoped my animals were ok. The neighbor was supposed to go get them.

My attorney was waiting outside Sybil Brand when I was released, ready and waiting to give me a ride and offer me money to pay my rent if I slept with him. Straight out of jail, my only hope was a John or the strip club.

I called a club manager, went by the house, and gathered my costume bag. When I walked in, I had forgotten how dark it was in that place in contrast with the light outside. This was the first time I was drug-free entering a club since I auditioned at the bikini bar a decade ago. As I found my way through the crowd, I noticed the smells I had just grown used to, like stale mildew carpet, alcohol, cigarettes, and cigars. I walked through the curtains into the dressing room, where the smell of weed, body sprays, body oils, hair spray, and feet hit me. I set my things down on the makeup counter. I went to the DJ booth, gave him some music for my first set, and returned to the dressing room to get ready.

I sat down at the makeup counter and looked in the mirror. How far away I had gotten from that 19-year-old girl who bravely got on the plane almost 11 years ago. I didn't see her now. I lost her a long time ago somewhere along this road. And now, after prison, I didn't even see Kori anymore. Who was it looking back at me now? I looked around at the other girls; no one seemed to notice I was having a moment. There were some new faces in the dressing room and some familiar ones. Some I had seen on rotation for years…like me. I wondered for the first time; how long WILL women do this for? How long CAN they do this? How long can I do this? I remembered seeing a 50-year-old woman dancing at one of the dives way back in those early days when I first started dancing. She probably didn't plan on doing it that long, either. But she couldn't pull out of the quicksand. As I looked around the club, I felt sick. I can't.

I JUST CAN'T DO THIS ANYMORE.

I got up and walked through the curtains that go out on "the floor." You aren't supposed to go out unless you are in costume and in hair and makeup. I stood there looking around.

I looked at the men sitting on the stage and then at the men in the back of the room getting lap dances. Everyone looked so revolting. I approached the DJ booth and told him to take me off the rotation. He was confused. "Are you going home because it's your birthday?"

"Nope, I am quitting," was all I could say. I went into the dressing room and gave away all of my costumes. The girls grabbed whatever they wanted, saying, "There's no way you're quitting for real; you'll be back." I looked at my empty costume bag lying on the floor…then I turned and walked out of the club for the last time. I quit the club on June 6, 1994, my 30th birthday. It was the greatest gift I could give to myself, the gift of discovering I'm worth so much more! I walked over to a cab waiting out in the parking lot for drunk customers and opened the door. I'm not sure how long I stood looking at the entrance door of the club. "Hey, are you getting in?" the driver asked, breaking me out of my thoughts. "Yep. I'm ready." As we drove out of the parking lot, I whispered a prayer: "God, if you can use me to help these girls get out, I'll come back."

I turned and walked out of the club for the last time.

...

QUESTIONS: UNLOCKING THE CAGE

1. If you could do whatever you wanted as a career and money wasn't an issue, what would you do?

2. What obstacle stands in your way?

3. It takes a lot of courage to change things. What about your life would you want to be different?

4. Are your choices moving you closer or further away from your goals?

CHAPTER 20

THE GIRL IN THE NEON MARTINI GLASS (FLASHBACK)

"No one could know how that night
would change the course of my life."

...

watched the neon sign of the club fade out of sight, and as I sat in the back seat of the cab, a long-lost memory of another neon sign came to mind. One I had long forgotten, one I saw at five years old of a nude girl in a martini glass.

I don't have that many memories of my dad, but the few I do are so vivid.

I can still hear his car pulling in slowly up the back driveway late in the night, tires crunching over rocks as he parked under the carport. I was five years old. The back door, which led directly into my bedroom, would creak open, followed by the rattle of glass as he shut the door behind him. The stench of alcohol and cigarettes always surrounded him. My heart pounded as I smelled him approaching and getting closer.

I could feel the warmth of his breath and the strong odor of alcohol as he leaned in close to look at me. I would lay so still, paralyzed, and pretend to be asleep. My mom called it "playing possum," but this didn't feel like a game.[4] It was the only way I knew how to escape his drunkenness. Most times I was filled with so much excitement when I saw him. He loved to play with me on Saturdays when he was working in the yard, but at night when he came home, I remember feeling terrified.

I hoped he couldn't see or hear my heart pounding out of my chest. He paused for what felt like a long time, standing over me. Thankfully, I finally felt him move away from my bed and stumble out of the room, and I could let out the breath I had been holding in and breathe again.

My parents had five children. Four children perfectly spaced two years apart, they would be close in age. But then, 12 years later, to her dismay, she found out she was pregnant again. She was never planning to have another child.

Mother was 44, and Daddy, 57, and neither wanted to start again with another child. My mother later told me that I wouldn't have been born if it had been up to my dad. He wanted her to have an abortion, but she was adamantly opposed to the idea based on her religious beliefs, and abortions were illegal.

From what she told me about their relationship, I think my mom had "played possum" many nights too. But on the nights she couldn't pretend to sleep, they ended up in terrible fights. Later in her old age, she confided in me that she "spent most nights sleeping on

---

4 *"Playing possum" is now recognized as a trauma response when someone involuntarily enters a catatonic state.*

the couch to avoid him, and the night that I had been conceived was when he was drunk and forced her to against her will."[5]

What a punch in the gut that was! All these years of being told you were a "surprise baby" to suddenly and so nonchalantly hear the real narrative: you were a child of rape, unwanted. But that explains a lot! There are studies done on trauma in the womb and its effect on unwanted children.

Even as a child, I could see her unhappiness; as time went on, it became clear to me by her tone she resented us both; him for the violation and me for reminding her of him.

That same night she told me about my conception, my mother unburdened herself of a few other dark secrets she had been carrying, and she let on that there were more by the way she hinted at things that she didn't fully share. That makes me sad that she took them to her grave and that she was never able to be fully free. That is another kind of torture.

One night, I woke up to my mother talking on the green phone attached to the wall in the hallway just outside my bedroom door. A few minutes later, she rushed into my room. "Get up!" she said. Sleepy-eyed and scared, I couldn't understand what was happening, but I could tell she was mad, and I knew enough not to make her ask me a second time. She pushed me to put on my robe and slippers, "Hurry up," she said through gritted teeth.

Off we went into the night, still wondering where we were going, but Mama was silent. You could always tell when she was mad by her eyes; she had a look that said it all.

---

5 Rape within a marriage is considered spousal rape or marital rape when one person does not consent. It wasn't considered illegal and allowed for prosecution until the 1970s.

"Hurry up," she said through gritted teeth. Off we went into the night.

...

I could see that we were headed downtown near the railroads. I knew this was an area where we didn't go often, especially at night. There weren't any streetlights or anything else, just old, closed warehouses. Suddenly, we turned down a side street, and she pulled over to the side of the road and turned off the car.

I jumped in the back seat and peeked out the window. The only thing lighting up the night was the flashing neon sign; it was the outline of a girl sitting in a giant martini glass. The neon lights going on and off made her legs look like she was kicking them up and down as they hung out of the glass.

After a few minutes, I saw the door open, and my dad stumbled outside. Daddy didn't see us. Mama rolled down the window and angrily yelled his name. "Armand!"

I sank down on the floorboard to hide. I didn't want him to know I had seen him this way.

So, this is where he goes when he's not home with us, I thought. *This must be what makes him happy.*

My mom didn't seem to remember I was in the car, or maybe she didn't care that I had seen him drunk or that he knew that I had seen him in this state. But I felt ashamed and scared for having seen him like this. She also didn't seem to care if I saw how angry and mean she was to him. Her face was tight with disgust, and her words came out sharp to cut him down to size. I felt sorry for him and helpless to protect him from her anger.

When he got in the car, a plume of cigarette smoke and the stench of alcohol came with him. I stayed as quiet as I could on the floor of the back seat so he wouldn't notice me. I felt scared seeing him drunk. What was it about drinking and going to this place with the neon girl in the martini glass that made him happy? On Saturdays, when he was home, he seemed happy when I followed him around the backyard, "helping" him pick tomatoes and cucumbers from the garden he had planted. He seemed happy when he pushed me on the tree swing that he had made for me in our backyard.

My dad was a talented musician and could play all kinds of instruments—the piano, organ, violin, brass (trombone & horn), harmonica—and all by ear.

But he loved jazz and big band most.

I would sit and stare at the covers of his jazz albums for what seemed like hours, looking at every detail of the women featured on them and thinking how beautiful they looked—their hair, skin, make-up, clothes, or lack thereof. I figured they must be good singers because they were on the album covers. My love for music came from him.

Years ago, in the army, he played the trombone for the band.

Mother would tell me a story about how, in the early days, the 1940s, she and Dad would go out to the USO, the dance hall for the enlisted men, and one time, she said Dad played with the band, she was proud of that—it was really the only time I heard her say something kind about him, the only time she permitted me to be proud of him, too. Back then, there were supper clubs with big bands and live music, and my mother loved to dance. Before she married, she often went with the enlisted men my grandmother set her up with. Grandmother would make big Sunday dinners and invite many of the boys to eat and meet her available daughters. She often reminisced about those days with fond memories of the boys in uniform.

One she would talk about was a pilot she dated. She would openly say she regrated not marrying him. He gave her a clock and wrote a poem about their time apart and waiting for him until he returned. He never made it home, and she would imagine how her life would have been different had she married him.

Even though I loved seeing her face light up when she remembered being young, beautiful, and in love, I always felt sad that she wasn't happy now.

Mama loved the *real* classic movies, the 40s and 50s classics. Fred Astaire and Ginger Rogers, Gene Kelly, Bing Crosby, Danny Kaye, Esther Williams, Doris Day, and Rock Hudson were just a few of her favorites. I loved watching those movies with her; sometimes, during commercials (yes, we had to watch commercials), she would dance with me and teach me the steps, like the jitterbug. Those were the rare times I saw her smile and laugh; she seemed almost young again.

I fell in love with dancing and the fashion of that era because of her.

During the War, my dad was stationed in Okinawa. After the War, things got tough for families and for soldiers returning home. The men were different when they came home. They had seen and experienced things that most civilians could never fathom. Most of them brought back physical and psychological traumas and suffered severely from PTSD, though, in that era, there was not a lot of help for them. Some of the returning men couldn't cope, and many committed suicide. Others tried to drown their pain in a bottle. My dad was one of them.

Dad's drinking didn't get better over time. It got worse, from what she would say. He was a mean drunk, she would tell me.

Once during one of their fights, my mother changed all the locks on the house while he was out so he couldn't come back home, but eventually, she let him back in. I always wanted to know more about him, the good and the bad, but when I would ask for anything, just something to hold onto, the response would always be the same: he was mean, or he was "just awful."

But every little girl wants to know about her dad. Whenever I asked about him, she would become furious that I wanted to know, and then I would get the silent treatment, leaving me to fill in the blanks with my own experience of him and the data I could put together from pictures.

Sometimes, he'd go to church with us, usually on holidays. Going to church with the whole family for Easter and Christmas allowed me to pretend everything was normal. I'd sit between my daddy and Mama and rest my head on his arm. I was little and couldn't reach his shoulder.

As it turned out, I never would.

We were taught in the South that divorce was an unpardonable sin. There was no other option for women suffering domestic violence but to stick it out, and I would hear her say that all she could do was to pray that out of the two of them, he would go first.

Before I would turn six, she would get the answer to her prayer.

QUESTIONS: THE GIRL IN THE NEON MARTINI GLASS

1. Do you have a specific young memory that lingers, even haunts you, that you have never felt safe enough to talk about?

2. If you had a safe person that could help you see the ways in which this early memory is playing out in your present-day life, would you go there?

3. How often do you have a flashback or memory intrusion and begin to disassociate from the present, and do you recognize when it is happening?

CHAPTER 21

SEPTEMBER
(FLASHBACK)

"That had been my only role in this
family, the little entertainer. But no
one laughed or said anything."

...

It was 9/11/1969. I heard their voices, arguing, growing louder and louder. I crouched deeper under the covers, trying to hide. I felt scared.

As soon as I thought it was safe, I ran into the hallway, but was quickly shooed back in a bedroom. There was a full-size bed high off the floor, and the walls were covered in blue and white flowered wallpaper. A large mirror hung behind the door, and I would sometimes go in there to hide and play. I would stand in front of the mirror and pretend to be on stage singing with my hairbrush as my microphone. But this time I wasn't hiding in the room for fun.

At one point I heard the arguing in the hallway, and I ran out again to see what was going on.

My mom was blocking the bathroom doorway, while my dad was trying to get in. I saw in her face such rage and fear. I had seen it many times look that way. In that moment I felt scared of both of them. He stumbled toward her and she shoved him away. As if in slow motion, I watched as he fell backward on the metal furnace grate on the hallway floor. I was standing on the other side of the furnace, and seeing a grown man fall was scarier than anything I had seen. I saw the fear on her face as she slammed the bathroom door to keep him out. My heart broke for him and in that moment I felt so much hate for my mother! In my mind the fighting was her fault and I wondered how she could be so cruel to him?

I tried to ask what was going on, but no one would answer me. "Go back to sleep," and I finally did. But not for long, I woke up again and this time all the lights in the house were on. The only time I could remember everyone getting up early when it was still dark outside was when we would go on vacation to the beach. My dad loved to pack the car and leave for a trip while it was still dark. How I wished that was why everyone was up, but there was something very different going on and I felt afraid.

I slipped off the high bed onto the floor and quietly stood in the doorway watching my mother move from the bedroom to the bathroom to get hot and cold washcloths for my father's head. All I could hear now was him cussing from the severe pain. Everyone seemed so afraid and I saw them crying—but not my mother. She didn't cry. I have never seen her cry. Ever.

She always said she never had been able to cry. And she didn't tolerate it either, even if she was the one to make me cry. Whenever I cried, she'd tell me I had better stop crying or she'd "give me something to cry about!" Or she would say "oh you're just a crybaby." Now, seeing my sisters crying, I blurted out to them, "Stop being a crybaby!" I wanted them to yell at me, do something, but just include me, tell me what's going on!

No matter what age, when the mind can't understand, the body will still hold the story.

My little 5-year-old body could feel immense fear, and I wanted to understand why.

Lights flashed against the blue and white flowered papered walls. Strange men rushed into our house. Every muscle in my body tightened as I was kept out of the way. My dad had died of a cerebral hemorrhage. The gurney rolled past my bedroom door. I could see the outline of my dad's figure laying there under the sheet.

As the gurney rolled by, I felt so scared. I didn't understand but it felt like *I* needed to do something. I needed to change the atmosphere. I didn't want to feel whatever this was, it was too much. Seeing the sheet over the outline of the body, it reminded me of the communion table at the front of the church on Sundays, so I blurted out, "Are we going to have communion?"

Trying to get someone to respond, to notice me standing there witnessing this horror scene.

My way of doing that was to get them to laugh (that had been my role in this family, the little entertainer). But no one laughed or said anything.

It was like I was invisible, a bystander. But I wasn't a bystander; this was MY dad!

I knew he loved me and he wouldn't want to leave me!

I knew he loved me and he wouldn't want to leave me!

...

I had no idea it would be the last time I would ever see him. In that moment, in a whirlwind of horror and panic, my life would be redirected…forever!

I don't remember when they finally told me he was dead. I think they waited. I wasn't allowed to attend the funeral. Instead of taking me with the rest of the family to bury him, to say goodbye, Mother sent me to the neighbor's house down the street. Having me there at the funeral was probably too much of a risk for everyone, who knows what I would have said.

The only way I could deal with how alone and confused I felt was to create another reality about my dad's death. Up until my teen years, I told myself and wanted to believe that my father had faked his own death to get away from my mother. After all, I had seen and heard how she treated him.

I imagine there were things he wanted to escape, like his memories of the war and who knows what else? Not being able to follow his dreams of music and the things that truly made him happy. Maybe he had trauma from his own childhood—abuse, neglect, loneliness? What about his dreams? Maybe that's why he drank—to forget, to drown the pain.

But regardless, I adored him, and I studied all the things that *he* loved: music, gardening, dancing—and from the album covers, beautiful women.

In my experience of him, I felt that he loved and delighted in his little Katiedid.

He worked at the post office, and Mother would dress me up and take me to his job to see him. We would drive in the back way where the mail trucks pulled into the loading docks, and then he'd come out and lift me up to the upper level where he was. It seemed so high, and when he grabbed me and pulled me up it was such a thrill. Then he'd walk around and show me off to all his friends at work.

I couldn't make sense of why he'd want to leave if he loved me so much. I imagined that he went off to play his music—that was his real love—and that he thought about me but couldn't contact me. Like we had a secret, and my plan was to go find him. Maybe he went to New York or LA.

I made a vow and told myself, *when I grow up, I'm going to those places where he might have gone and I'm going to follow him into the music world and make him proud of who I've become. I'll follow in his footsteps into the entertainment business, and he'll hear about me and be proud. He'll come and find me. We'll be together again, and I won't have to be lonely anymore.*

Children don't have the language for grief, especially at a time of trauma and loss. Studies have shown that by age two, a child can already "read" the adults in their life.[6] And because they do, and tell the truth, these children are labeled as "too much" or "precocious" when they see and say what's happening. They are too often dismissed and shuffled off in order not to expose something of the family and/or cause the family some level of embarrassment. But the truth is, more than anyone, the child needs to experience the security of their caregivers, and they need to borrow language from them to process and name the truth of what they are experiencing—which is an ending. An unexpected, violent, abrupt ending—a profound loss at such a young age.

If we are not taught how to do endings well, then they are experienced as abandonment.

6 Schnarch, David. "Brain Talk." *CreateSpace, Evergreen, CO* (2018).

I would spend the next thirty years looking for the affirmation of my dad.

QUESTIONS: SEPTEMBER

1. What was your "role" growing up as a child? Scapegoat, golden child, clown, or lost child are just a few.

2. Who was with you when you first experienced grief?

3. How did you process it?

CHAPTER 22

WATER FOUNTAINS (FLASHBACK)

"Never enough and always too much."

...

started first grade ten months after my dad died. When we walked into the school building, I remember the strong smell of pine sol and old books. My teacher looked mean and scary, and older like my mother. She wore gray dresses most of the time and rarely smiled at me. I got the feeling on the first day that she didn't like me. Maybe it was because we were poor and she could see my clothes were homemade. Whatever it was, the message was already clear: I wasn't good enough.

I was the child whose father had recently died and whose mother was old enough to be my grandmother. I felt so much shame.

I wanted to show her she was wrong about me, that I had good manners and was an obedient child so that she would like me. One day, she announced to the class to line up to get a drink at the water fountain, which was inside the classroom. I was first in line. There was a cute boy that all the girls were already forming a crush on named Jimmy, and he was standing in line right behind me. I was so excited to be near him. I secretly hoped that the teacher would decide to make us partners.

I was also excited to be in line for the drinking fountain because I had not been allowed to use a water fountain in public. Ever. It was 1970 in Albany, Georgia, and in the South, public drinking fountains were still separated by a sign over them that read "White" or "Colored." Even though the Jim Crow laws had been abolished five years earlier, the water fountains were physically and mentally a reminder that change was not going to come about easily.

I was excited that *everyone* was invited to line up at the fountain… together! But when I stepped up to the sink, I was confused. Never having been allowed to drink out of a public water fountain, I didn't know what to do. I had only been allowed to use the kids' fountain at my all-white Presbyterian church. I'd never seen a public fountain like this one. It was a sink with two different water spigots. On one side, there was a taller fountain, and on the other side, a smaller one.

Being first in line I desperately wanted to make a good impression to set the way. I thought maybe they were for smaller people and taller people. Not for Black or White? I was wearing a dress, so I reasoned I would use the taller side so I wouldn't have to bend over too far. When the teacher saw me, she yelled, "No! Not like that! That side isn't for you!"

I was confused by her anger and scared now that I could see how easily her wrath erupted.

She pushed me out of the way and told Jimmy to go first, keeping her hand on my shoulder, forcing me back in line behind a few other kids. Now, everyone was making fun of me. I had wanted to lead the way and had failed, and if there was any chance at making new friends, that just flew out the window when everyone became angry at me for breaking in line. Their faces reflected hers telling me I was stupid for drinking water from the wrong side of the fountain.

Soon, I made friends with a girl named Blessing. She was the only Black girl in my class. I approached her at recess one day and asked her to play. She wore her hair in what seemed like a hundred beautiful braids, each in a neat row with so many beautiful, different-colored butterfly and bow-shaped barrettes at the end of each braid. I was fascinated at how neat the rows were, and how beautiful she looked wearing her hair like that. Every day we played together at recess, just us two, and had so much fun! We made a pact that we would be best friends.

When I got home, I asked my momma if Blessing could come over to play after school the next day. She laughed out loud at the thought and said no I could not invite her to come over. I remember crying and being so angry at my mother, knowing what her reason was. I went and hid, with hot salty tears rolling down my cheeks, and whispered how much I hated my mother for not letting me have her as a friend.

I didn't care what she said. We might not be able to go over to each other's houses, but we were friends no matter what anyone else said. That night I gathered all my barrettes to wear my hair like hers, and the next morning I went to the mirror and started to put them in my hair just like hers. Well, not exactly, but I did the best I could. I'm sure it looked a mess and when mama saw me, she went into a rage. Instead of talking to me about appropriate hair styles for me, she just pulled all of the barrettes out of my hair and said "You're not going to wear your hair like a—" I'm not going to repeat the word she used.

After "teaching me a lesson" with the whip for screaming about it, she brushed my hair so hard, every stroke a punishment. It was so painful as the brush grated and dug into my scalp—then she pulled it back into the tightest ponytail like she always did when she was mad at me, and I couldn't help but cry. I remember always having the worst headaches from her hair rages, and there were many.

One day I surprised her when she made me go with her to get her hair done. While she was under the dryer, I asked for a haircut, a very short pixie. I remember the feeling of watching as the lady cut off my long hair, and watching all that hair (and all those beatings) hit the floor.

I found no joy in learning; there was nothing positive about any experience I had.

I continually asked, "How many more days of school are left?" Every day that passed meant I was closer to being done for that year. I barely got through each year with a passing grade. Mother never really could help me with school. She'd get frustrated trying to explain something to me, which she probably didn't understand herself, and I'd end up feeling like it was my fault that I was struggling and felt stupid because I couldn't understand.

I later learned that she had dropped out of high school to work at the post office with her dad. No wonder at 55 she struggled to help me with my homework.

Not long after starting second grade, something happened that would plant a lie in me that I still have to contend with. My teacher called my mom to schedule an after-school meeting. I was worried about my mom coming to school. Whenever we would go out in public together, I was often asked if she was my grandmother. This made me feel so ashamed and embarrassed. I felt like people were staring at us all the time. I wished she was young, and I wanted them to say my mother was pretty. I needed something to take away the shame of being a bad student and having an old mother. I felt so exposed.

Later at home after the meeting with my teacher that day, I overheard my mother on the phone telling her friend Doris about what the teacher had called her in to discuss; she told her that I might not be ready for third grade.

I was so embarrassed and ashamed. I already felt like I wasn't smart enough and now this made me feel even more hopeless. Why would she tell anyone what my teacher had said?

Ever since my dad died, I had often overheard my mom telling people how hard it was for her at her age to "start all over again." I can't even begin to count the number of times I heard her say this! Let me just note that my relationship with my mother was very different than that of any of my other siblings. She was older when she was parenting me. I was born under different circumstances and now she was a widow in her fifties going through menopause, starting over with a child she described as "a lot" (in other words, "too much"). Anyone who knew my mother would tell you what a great and kind woman she was. And it is true. Even more so after someone passes, they seem to be made into a saint. That is how she is remembered by everyone.

But it is also true how while I witnessed my mother's ability to be kind and offer care to others endlessly, my personal experience of her as an older single mother was very different. She was tired and angry, and no matter how you justify it, the "spankings" were abusive.

I say this with much ambivalence.

My feelings for my mother were always confusing. I loved her and I needed her approval and I also often despised her. When she died, the night before the funeral, I drank too much and cried more than I ever had in my life for the loss of her. But I was also grieving the loss of a relationship I never fully had.

My feelings for my mother were always confusing. I loved her and I needed her approval and I also often despised her.

...

Sometimes our "loyalty" toward our families keeps us silenced from working through our own true feelings. No one wants the family to be exposed, so we keep up the appearances, stick to a script, a polite narrative—and yet everyone, if they are honest, feels these kinds of emotions at some point. It's normal.

Not long after that meeting with the teacher, Mother told me she had made an appointment to see a doctor in Atlanta. I had had an allergic reaction to going barefoot in the grass every summer, and I thought that might be why she was taking me to a doctor. She never said what the reason was, only that he was a doctor. The drive from Albany to Atlanta was at least three hours, which meant we were up before daybreak to get ready for the trip. Instead of this feeling like the kind of exciting adventure my dad would take us on for family vacations to the beach, this trip felt scary. I knew I was the reason we had to take this trip, but I didn't understand what it was about— only that the problem was me. I felt like a dark cloud was always looming over me.

My mother was particular about how I looked when we went out, so the ritual for our trip began the night before with rolling my hair tight on sponge rollers and laying out my clothes—a dress, red tights, patent leather shoes. Only my Sunday best clothes for a doctor's appointment. I dreaded the morning because I knew what was coming. Sleeping on the rollers was so painful, I always woke up in pain and tired.

I could sense her mood by the way she shouted my name: "KATE! Come here and let me fix your hair." The *way* she said my name when she was angry. I hated the sound of my name. I decided that name belonged to someone dumb and ugly—someone unwanted.

I walked into her bedroom so she could take out the rollers hoping today might be different.

It would always begin the same way every time with her pulling my hair so hard, I'd cry. "OUCH! You're hurting me!" As soon as the words came out, I knew the beating would begin.

Just like she had done in the past, she started brushing and pulling so hard hair was coming out. I wondered why she even had me wear rollers if she was going to brush all the curls out.

If I pulled away in pain, that's when she would hit me with the brush, threatening that I had better stop crying. But it was impossible not to cry. The more she pulled at my hair, the more intense the pain became. She would grab my arm and hold me tightly so I couldn't get away from her. In between each lash, in a rhythmic tone that coincided with each whip, she would repeat: "Didn't- I-Tell-You-Not-To-Move!!" The hairbrush stung so bad, each lash left huge red welts on my legs, butt, and sometimes my back.

I squirmed and twisted to try to loosen her grip, and when I finally broke free, I ran!

This had truly become a ritual between us. Things were going to get worse.

She chased me, hitting me anywhere the brush could reach. More than once, the fury didn't end until it had reached its climax and her weapon, the hairbrush, or ruler, had broken. On this morning as we prepared to go to the doctor appointment, she yelled in a sharp voice over her shoulder as she left me crying, "You had better learn how to act!" I collapsed on the floor sobbing and rubbing the welts, thankful to be wearing red tights.

I think the doctor appointment proved to be unsuccessful in the sense that nothing changed after it. If I did need medication, she didn't agree to it. It was seen as shameful. But I would rather have been understood. If I had been diagnosed with ADHD or any form of the spectrum, I would have at least had a name for "being different." Today everyone is so much more educated about mental health and I am so thankful for that.

I didn't end up failing or needing to repeat my grade. I did, however, develop deep shame around my inability to succeed in school. All these years later, that narrative of shame—that I was different, that I wasn't smart enough—would haunt me and hold me back from believing I was ever going to "be enough" while also always being "too much."

Looking back, I'm shocked that no one thought to address the trauma I had experienced in witnessing my dad's violent death at five years old. My brain felt like tangled spaghetti trying to make sense of what had happened, and not talking about it added to the shame I felt. Of course, I was struggling at school! I could barely think about anything else except missing my dad and finding him when I got older.

> Looking back, I'm shocked that no one thought to address the trauma I had experienced in witnessing my dad's violent death at five years old.

...

QUESTIONS: WATER FOUNTAINS

1. Have you ever felt like you were too much? Who told you that?

2. Have you felt like you were not good enough? If you think about it, who's voice comes to mind?

CHAPTER 23

SPIRITUAL SOUP

"Only at the time, I didn't know what
kind of rescue I really needed."

. . .

wasn't sure what I would do after prison, but I remembered another
dancer, Stacy, who had told me that she and her husband were
opening a bookstore and needed someone to work there. It sounded
perfect. After all, finding a job after working as a dancer for the past ten
years wouldn't be easy. The only legitimate experience I could include
on a resume was my earlier work as a skilled stylist and licensed cosmetologist. But returning to salon work would mean starting over at the
bottom, doing shampoos at minimum wage for a younger hairdresser
who had less experience than me. Even though I had worked at top
salons in the past, I was still going to be new and start at the bottom
as a shampoo assistant AT MINIMUM WAGE!

I was screwed.

The thought of starting over in a salon felt humiliating and
degrading, given all my prior experience working for Sebastian and
Christine Valmy before coming to LA. The beauty school I graduated

from is one of the best in the nation. Even though my work at the clubs was humiliating and degrading on a different scale compared to returning to the beauty industry, where it is all about respect, I couldn't bring myself to do it. I wanted to return to being a stylist, but I couldn't afford to live off $8 an hour, not in LA! The problem I kept running into, though, was filling out job applications. How would I account for the past decade on my resume?

When I look at this list of clubs, I am shocked to see how many there were. I had no idea. No wonder I was so tired. It is true the first thing a survivor needs when leaving the industry is rest!

If you could see my resume, there is a 10-year span of working in the industry, which would be a considerable gap that I had to explain. As you will learn later, that is the main reason I started a social enterprise to help girls have recent job training to add to a resume.

Stacy invited me to her home for drinks and to discuss working at her bookstore. When I arrived, she poured me a glass of wine and gave me a quick tour of her home. I noticed in the spare room a giant three-dimensional pyramid made from copper pipes sitting in the center of the room on the floor. I thought it was a sculpture or an art project still in progress. "Ooh, what's this?" I asked excitedly. "It's going to hang over our bed," said Stacy. "It will make us more enlightened." Okay, I thought that seemed odd, but I guess it could be worse. Stacy and her husband seemed nice enough, and they weren't judging or hassling me for quitting the industry. I was surprised by this. Usually, someone who wanted to meet with me had another motive for getting together. It was always something to keep you in the industry—an "escort" job to entice you to stay, a friend (businessman) looking to hire a girl as a companion for a trip somewhere, or a need for a date to an executive party. It was always some side job that included big money to tempt you, but you'd usually end up in bed. I was done with that life. Soon after our dinner, I went to the bookstore. I was relieved to see that they were selling books! They carried various products, mostly related to "spiritual enlightenment," including oils and other herbs for mixing and sage for burning.

Stacy knew I was creative. She had seen all the jewelry and costumes I had made to sell to the girls working in the clubs. She asked me if I would like to paint something out front on the vast shop window—something for people to see and intrigue them to enter the store. I didn't consider myself a painter, but I said I'd try it. I decided to paint the tree from my childhood front yard with the purple wisteria vine taking over. It felt like an homage to my childhood, a remembrance of my innocence, which I longed to feel again but that seemed so far away, like a dream. One evening, Stacy and I were working at the store together. A local from the neighborhood, originally from France, frequently popped his head in when I was working to say, "Bonjour!" On this night, I was helping Stacy hang a bunch of flowers upside down on the wall to dry them. This man saw what we were doing through the window and burst through the door to stop us, nearly knocking me off the ladder. "No! No! No!!" he yelled. And in French, he said something that translated to, "Life, not death!" "Don't hang the flowers upside-down!" he continued. "Only hang them upside-down when there is a death. You want to bring life." I had heard a lot of superstitions and sayings growing up in the South, but I'd never heard that one.

He talked about random things, including his grandmother, who had died years ago. Stacy started asking him about his grandmother and whether he wished to speak to her. Suddenly, he began to cry. I was still on the ladder, and they were below me talking. I was watching this scene like an outside spectator. I began to feel uncomfortable, not because a stranger was emotional but because the conversation had suddenly taken a turn; they were discussing talking with a dead person! Stacy told him she could reach his grandmother, and he could say what he had missed out on speaking to her.

All these years, I had been trying to convince myself that all spiritually was okay, leading to seeking truth. I thought everyone was going about it in their own way, and God would be okay with how we found our way to him. But in this moment, I sensed I was in the presence of something that was not truth. It felt dark. I felt a wave of nausea coming over me. This eerie feeling of another presence in the room wasn't new. I had felt it before, but this time I knew what it was. I was not in a fog of darkness anymore. Light was beginning to come into my life, and I felt the opposition. He and Stacy went into the back of the store and sat down. Stacy lit a candle and incense. She told him to close his eyes and concentrate on his memories of his grandmother, to call for his grandmother. He began wailing louder and louder for her to come to be with him. Suddenly I heard a strange voice, a woman speaking French. It was Stacy's voice.

I didn't know she spoke French! Stacy was channeling his grandmother. I decided it was time to leave. I finished my work quickly, cleaned up, and left without saying anything to Stacy or Jean. When I woke the next day, I saw that Stacy had called my pager several times. I still felt sick, like something was going wrong. I was worried about going back to the store the next day. I didn't want to work for a psychic. I didn't know that she was so deep into the occult. How would I tell her I was freaked out and didn't want to work there anymore? I was nervous, but I called to see what was going on. She began yelling at me and accusing me of stealing oils from her shop.

She said if I showed my face there, I would get arrested. She was taking out a restraining order. I couldn't believe it! The timing was all so strange. Only a few weeks ago, I had gotten out of jail with car theft on my record. Now, she was accusing me of stealing. I definitely couldn't show my face at her shop again. I left that job and never looked back. I believe God got me out of there. He rescued me again!

QUESTIONS: SPIRITUAL SOUP

1. When have you made a decision to do something new and different, where you trusted someone and hoped the results would be a better choice for you, but you ended up in another relationship or friendship betrayal?

2. Have you ever had an experience with the spirit world, practiced witchcraft, or been in a cult realm?

CHAPTER 24

UNDONE

"He led me to a place of safety; He rescued
me because he delighted in me."

• • •

(PSALMS 18:19 NLT)

So how does a girl who was stuck in the quicksand of sexual exploitation for a decade change her whole life over to helping those out of the same pit she was in? Only by God! It was only by God that I lived to get out and have a second chance.

A vision began to form in my mind to start a non-profit to offer rest and restoration to women who have survived a life of sexual exploitation like me. I would call it Cherished because these women were my beloved sisters, and like God had chased after me, He would chase after them too. He was sending me to show them they are Cherished, because I know their pain that keeps them bound, and I don't want anyone to go through what I have been through. He rescued me and called me to tell my story because He loves us. He pointed me to a Scripture to tell me how he saw me: "He led me to a place of safety; He rescued me because he delighted in me" (Psalms 18:19 NLT).

I had to meditate on that for a while, especially the part that says he "delighted in me." That couldn't be true, not for me or after all I had done. My mind flashed back to a time when I was the perpetrator. I played the role of pimp/madam. A wealthy client had hired me to gather five other girls to go on a weekend trip on his yacht to Catalina Island to serve his business partners. Although the women agreed to go, still I was the recruiter. I had made money by causing harm and exploitation too. I felt such a self-contempt. It was hard to see how God might not see me through the same lens. Every time I had a flashback, I would have to remind myself again about the night I felt God's presence in my little room in N. Hollywood on Magnolia St. That night everything changed for me.

My true God encounter moment came while I was still working in the clubs. I had been trying to summon up courage again for a while. I looked down at my ankle and saw my tattoo. It is the courage symbol inside of a sun. The sun had a double meaning for me. I also represented the "s-o-n." I thought about that. I was writing on my body a literal message "have COURAGE in the SON" Meaning TRUST. As I pondered that I felt such a peace in my room. Suddenly a wave came over me, and it hit me. I fell to my knees; I saw that God had been with me since I was a little girl. I don't know why it happened then. I began to see his heart for me and how it was broken over me. Me! The God of the universe had a broken heart over me! My heart could feel what he felt about me, I could feel how much he loved me, and I was overwhelmed when I saw how he wept for me over the years. All of my self-hatred and the harm that I had suffered at the hands of others had broken HIS heart. And if what I felt was only a little of what He feels for me... I was UNDONE! God was not angry with me but instead felt so much love and joy over me that he would say He feels "delight" for me.

I could not stop weeping!

That moment was a game changer, and I would hold it in my heart, wondering how he would use me now that he was calling me to use that to fuel my purpose.

I wanted other survivors to know this message is for them too. As hard as it was, I continued to return to the strip clubs I had worked in. How could I not go? I saw the women there as my sisters; we suffered the same bondage. How could I leave them there when I know what they are going through? I made it my mission to tell them there was a way out. I got out, and if they wanted to, I was a hand to grab onto.

No one in my church knew what I had been through. All they knew about me is that I had joined the church, started serving in the Women's Ministry, attended regularly, and had become the wedding coordinator. I didn't think anyone could really handle me. My story was too much, so I smiled and suffered in silence. Until I couldn't any longer.

I realized my silence was keeping me in bondage, and I was mad at how much had been taken. I went to my pastor, Pastor Mark Goodell, and told him my story for the first time in 15 years. I told someone my story, and for the first time in my life, a man wept over everything I had been through. He wept over me. I was shocked! Men had been the abusers, predators, betrayers, and abandoners.

His tears and kindness were a new experience for me! I was expecting a little judgment, but that is not what I was met with. His tears made my heart soften, and I felt sad instead of ashamed and hateful.

Experts say the posttraumatic stress of a life of sexual exploitation is comparable to those who have endured combat in war. You experience aftershocks for the rest of your life. Today nearly 50 milllion people are victims of modern day slavery. Ninety percent of women trapped in the sex industry say they were sexually abused as children, while 87 percent say they would leave but had no other means of survival and 73 percent say they had been raped more than five times. Studies on the sex industry have shown that survivors have a high prevalence of PTSD. Sixty-eight percent of 827 survivors in nine countries met the criteria for a lifetime diagnosis of PTSD. The severity of PTSD symptoms in the participants was in the same range as treatment-seeking combat veterans.[7,8,9]

The needs for recovery are overwhelming. It takes a deep focus on complex trauma in particular and about 150 services to help a survivor on this journey. I knew we couldn't tackle every aspect of recovery right away, so we launched Cherished by focusing on walking with women on their healing journey, providing support groups and a healthy community for women. Not long after I decided to begin Cherished, things started happening. I was introduced to Trades of Hope, a fair-trade catalog that supports women all over the world to rise out of poverty by selling handmade items. I was asked if Cherished wanted to make jewelry to represent the USA in their international catalog. I loved that idea, and it was exactly one of the pillars I wanted to offer the women at Cherished.

7 Farley, Melissa, and Howard Barkan. "Prostitution, violence, and posttraumatic stress disorder." *Women & health* 27, no. 3 (1998): 37-49.

8 Kim, H. S. "Violent characteristics of prostitution and posttraumatic stress disorder of women in prostitution [Unpublished doctoral dissertation]." *Seoul: Sung-Gong-Hoe University* (2002).

9 Kaysen, Debra, Patricia A. Resick, and Deborah Wise. "Living in danger: The impact of chronic traumatization and the traumatic context on posttraumatic stress disorder." *Trauma, Violence, & Abuse* 4, no. 3 (2003): 247-264.

About that same time, I began to get asked to do speaking events, and one of them was to speak at a women's retreat. I had no idea what I would talk about. I knew people always want the details of the story, but I really wanted to share more about the journey to recovery.

I prayed and waited for God to tell me what to speak about, but he remained silent. For a year!

Some might have seen this as a sign that maybe they weren't called to continue the work they had begun. But I trusted God to give me something. After seeing all he had done and brought me out of, I wasn't going to let this scare me off. If you think He is telling you to do something, step out! Explore your faith!

Sure enough, at 4 am, one week before the event, I still had nothing. I woke up early and could not go back to sleep. I was worried about what I was going to do, and then I felt like I heard a voice say clearly. "Read Esther."

I immediately got out of bed and opened my Bible. I had read the book of Esther many times, but this time, in the early blue hour of the morning, I saw something I had never seen before: Esther had been trafficked! I felt like someone had knocked the wind out of me.

Here is the short version of her story.

A Persian king threw a huge party that lasted for months, inviting all the most important royals and nobles from all over to come. He wanted to impress them with his trophy wife, the beautiful queen. He commanded her to come out and entertain his guest with her nudity by stripping. When she refused, he became angry and humiliated and was advised to behead her for her disobedience. But a few days later, after sobering up, the king realized what he had done and he began brooding over the loss of Queen Vashti, realizing that he would never see her again.

His aids convinced him to send them out through the land to take young girls from their homes and families and bring them back to the palace to be his concubines. Then he could find another girl to bring him pleasure.

A man in one of the proveniences had a beautiful and lovely young cousin, Hadassah whose father and mother were dead, and whom he had adopted into his family and raised as his own daughter. Hadassah was captured and brought to the King's harem along with many other young girls and their names were changed to Persian names. Hadassah became Esther.

Hegai, a eunuch, was placed in charge of the harem. The instructions concerning these girls were that before being taken to the King's bed, each would be given six months of beauty treatments with oil of myrrh, followed by six months with special perfumes and ointments. Then, as each girl's turn came for spending the night with King Ahasuerus, she was given her choice of the clothing or jewelry she wished, to enhance her beauty. She was taken to the King's apartment in the evening and the next morning returned to the second harem where the King's wives and favorites lived.

When it was Esther's turn to go to the King, she accepted the advice of the eunuch in charge of the harem, dressing according to his instructions. The King loved Esther more than any of the other girls. He was so delighted with her that he set the royal crown on her head and declared her Queen instead of Vashti.

A concubine is a virgin who was trafficked and sold as a piece of property in the market or taken by force as part of a siege for the purpose of sex. Typically, being taken as a concubine was a violent and traumatic incident for the woman. Esther was an orphan raised by her cousin. She was very young, maybe 12 or 13, when she was forcefully taken from her home to become part of a harem. Her Jewish name, Hadassah, means Myrtle, which gives off its fragrance only when it's crushed. Esther, the Persian name she was given after becoming a concubine, means Hidden. The royal harem included three groups of women who lived in separate dwellings. First were the "ladies" of the household, legal wives other than the Queen, or the favorites of a noble house. The Queen, the ladies, and the favorites of the household would go to dinners with the King and dignitaries. Still, they would leave when "women entertainers" (other concubines) of the harem came in, and the men began merrymaking.

The second group consisted of unmarried and married princesses who lived with their own families in the palace. The third group of harem women were concubines, beautiful girls bought in slave markets, or received as a gift, or collected from different parts of the empire (Esther 2.2-3), and even captured from rebellious subjects. While still virgins, they were kept and groomed in the harem's "first house of women" (Esther 2.9). They were trained as musicians, dancers, and singers in order to entertain their King or the magnate lord at banquets or in the bedroom throughout the night. Historians say that as many as 300 women watched over the Persian King. They were taught a musical skill; "these women would sleep throughout the day in order to stay awake at night, but at night they sing and play on harps continually while the lamps burn; and the king takes his concubines."

The definition of Trafficking is the recruitment, use of force or other forms of coercion, abduction, fraud, deception, the abuse of power or of a position of vulnerability, or of the giving or receiving of payments or having control over another person for the purpose of exploitation.

Esther had been forced and taken to the King of Persia, whose purpose was to use her for his purposes. Often, we dismiss this by saying it was a cultural thing, but however you spin it, no young girl wants to be taken from her family, her tribe, to a foreign land to be used for sex. It's estimated that 44% of the world's population was ruled from the Achaemenid throne at that time. The book of Esther outlines the purification process the Persian empire used to indoctrinate the concubines and prepare them for the work they had been brought to do. For one year, the virgins were treated with oils to heal and calm them. First, they'd be treated with myrrh for six months, a sap that was used as one of the ingredients in the temple for holy anointing oils. It's also used in perfumes and in medicine for healing.

Myrrh is taken orally to treat arthritis, digestive discomfort, painful menstruation, respiratory infections, leprosy, syphilis, cancers, sore throats, asthma, coughs, and bad breath. Topically, myrrh has been used to treat muscular pains, arthritis, ulcers, sores, wounds, weak gums, loose teeth, bacterial and fungal skin infections, and acne; it's healing to the skin and an antiseptic for wounds. When Jesus was born, myrrh was offered as a gift from the Magi, likely as part of a treasure worth money, and served as an ancient "first aid kit" to his parents, Mary and Joseph. Myrrh with wine was also offered to Jesus as he hung on the cross to offer calm. He refused it and endured the full pain of his death by crucifixion.

Esther also received six months of treatment with sweet aromas. These would have included Frankincense, Lavender, Myrtle, and other oils. These oils provide a range of healing properties, such as aiding a youthful appearance, creating calmness, relieving stress, calming panic attacks, clearing acne, reducing puffiness and swelling, clearing warts, healing mouth ulcers, stopping hair loss, relieving anxiety, reducing insomnia, depression, muscle spasm, and migraines, relieving toothaches, nausea, and PMS symptoms, and enhancing overall psychological wellbeing. All the symptoms listed above are also symptoms of PTSD. What if Esther and her fellow concubine sisters also suffered PTSD like I and all the women at Cherished had? I was so inspired! I dressed immediately and drove for two hours to get the oils I needed. I bought labels, bottles, and seven different oils that were used on Hadassah and began to assemble oils to share with our Cherished women.

What if Esther and her fellow concubine sisters also suffered PTSD like I and all the women at Cherished had?

...

I had an amazing experience in Turkey recently when I got to go to the Sultan's palace. I saw the layout of the harem, the main room where the girls lived, the area where the eunuchs lived, the apartments for the favorites, and the Queen's separate quarters. The Hammam is the bath house or spa where the women would gather and stay all day receiving beauty treatments and care. I went and was so excited to be in the very place where many women before me, our ancestors and sisters, had gone. I felt kindred spirits in that place and understood why this place was so important to them. A place to feel safe and be with others who shared and understood the violations they had suffered.

But at the Hammam, sharing it with women who had not experienced that kind of exploitation, I felt uncomfortable. Maybe they had stories and maybe they did not—I would not know—but my body felt like I was in a familiar place but with strangers. For someone who has been exploited and had a lot of healing that needed to happen over my contempt for my own body, it was terrifying to undress and have eyes gazing again at my body. Entirely nude in a room of strangers. I cannot fully explain how it is that in this place, you are able to overcome and allow your body to relax. But I did.

To be cared for and touched in a non-sexual way—I don't have words. But my body experienced something very healing there that I had never had before.

I also walked through a Sultan's Palace and saw where there would have been private Hamams for the "favorites," where this kind of spa treatment would have happened. I thought about the women trafficked into the King's harem and how this would have been the only real safe space for their bodies to be thoroughly cared for and calmed.

As I studied Esther's story further, I noticed other parallels between her story and mine, as well as so many of the women at Cherished.

Here are three points to her story I could relate to:

1. Esther was an orphan, yet her lowly status didn't stop her from demonstrating great courage, mercy, and resolve on behalf of her people.
2. The evil plans of man were taken and used for good. She was being invited with dignity to serve God out of her pain. He didn't force her to do something she didn't want to do. When Esther was ready, she showed complete trust and faith in God. No matter what, she chose to follow the plan God had for her.

3. She was completely obedient to answer the call on her life, even though it was terrifying. She was brave, and because of this, she was able to help save an entire group of people from destruction. (This really spoke to me.)

These are the things that describe my work with Cherished.

We experience who we were created to be when we step boldly into our calling. We are ALL Esther.

The oils we were preparing for our Cherished women would remind them that their past circumstances had prepared them "for such a time as this." Just as God had used Esther's past to equip her for the call on her life, he was also redeeming our lives for his good purposes.

I couldn't wait to share the story of Esther at our Cherished retreat. Esther's life was a powerful way for them to see how their past circumstances could become the path to their glorious destiny.

The retreat was a big success! The women loved the connection between Esther's story and their own, and the oils provided a powerful, tangible way for them to embrace their courageous, redemptive story.

The oils I assembled at my kitchen table that first day eventually gave birth to a social enterprise for Cherished. Over time, we hired women in our program to help create Cherished-branded organic bath and body products. The oils' aromas created a sense of peace and calm in our workspace, and ultimately they aided in the women's healing process.

QUESTIONS: UNDONE

1. What are your thoughts about God?

2. Is He close by or far away?

3. Do you think He sees you?

4. Do you think He is angry with you?

5. Faith is believing what you cannot see. Did you know that *THE* God of the universe delights in YOU? It's really true! Ask Him about it.

6. Have you ever felt a higher power was watching over you?

7. What did you sense He/She felt about you?

CHAPTER 25

GOING UPSTREAM

"We need to stop just pulling people out
of the river. We need to go upstream
and find out why they're falling in."

• • •

DESMOND TUTU

Many people (sometimes even law enforcement) assume that if a woman is in the adult entertainment industry, she deserves everything that happens to her. Because they have "chosen" to make a living by getting paid to dance, strip, have sex, or be in adult films, they have no rights and don't deserve a voice. Ironically, often the people who believe women in the sex industry get what they deserve are often the same people who use pornography or go to strip clubs, taking what they want from women and never acknowledging how they're creating demand for and contributing to the problem of sexual exploitation of women.

"Choice" is actually a result of a lack of choices

· · ·

HARMONY/SURVIVOR

In 2016, Pornhub's year in review boasted 23 billion visits, 91,980,225,000 videos viewed. That is equal to 12.5 videos for every person on the planet.[10]

In 2017, Pornhub's year in review boasted of 28.5 billion visits. That's almost 1,000 visits a second. Totaling more than 4.6 billion hours of porn viewed in one year, the equivalent to 5,246 centuries. The most popular keywords for porn searches fell under the category of incest and included "stepmom," "mom," and "stepsister."[11]

In 2021, Pornhub announced 130 million site visits a day. In October of 2021, Facebook, Instagram, and WhatsApp were offline for several hours on October 4th, 2021. Starting at about 12 pm Eastern Time, Pornhub's traffic increased by as much as 10.5 percent, which equals about half a million additional users during each hour that Facebook's services were down.[12]

And it's not just young adult women that are targeted for online porn searches. Pornhub breaks down by state what people are looking for. During the Covid-19 pandemic, escort services became number one in the sex industry, with 150,000 new posts every minute!

10 *Pornhub's 2016 Year in Review*. (2017, January 4th). Pornhub Insights. Retrieved March 29th, 2023, from https://www.pornhub.com/insights/2016-year-in-review

11 *2017 Year in Review*. (2018, January 9th). Pornhub Insights. Retrieved March 29th, 2023, from https://www.pornhub.com/insights/2017-year-in-review

12 *2021 Year in Review*. (2021, December 14th). Pornhub Insights. Retrieved March 29th, 2023, from https://www.pornhub.com/insights/yir-2021

The people who consume pornography are choosing to soothe themselves by using the content of women being sexually exploited; they're perpetuating the cycle of sexual exploitation. In the book "Unwanted" by Jay Stringer, he discusses the key drives of porn use. He has many teaching books and guides to journey through unwanted sexual behavior and help understand how sexual brokenness formed.

Human trafficking is the second largest global organized crime today, generating approximately $150 billion USD each year. Statistics show 70 percent of females who are trafficked are sold into the commercial sex industry. Estimates show there are 4.5 million victims of commercial sexual exploitation worldwide. Trafficking for sexual exploitation generates approximately $99 billion USD per year. Exploitation is big business. It's far easier to blame the victims—the women who are enslaved in the sex industry—than it is for perpetrators of the sex industry to take responsibility for the choices they've made that have contributed to a nearly $100 billion industry that has destroyed the body, heart, and mind of millions of survivors worldwide. "Men and boys are also victimized by sex traffickers. LGBTQ boys and young men are seen as particularly vulnerable to trafficking."[13][14]

Survivors of the adult entertainment industry face a myriad of issues that impact their physical, emotional, and spiritual well-being and thwart their ability to leave the industry. For example, nearly 40 percent of women in the adult entertainment industry were victims of sexual abuse earlier in life. Before they ever had a choice, adults in their life robbed them of their innocence and dignity.

13 "Myths, Facts, and Statistics," *Polaris Project*, Accessed September 8, 2023, https://polarisproject.org/myths-facts-and-statistics/

14 International Labour Organization (ILO), Profits and Poverty: The Economics of Forced Labour, 2014, ISBN: 9789221287810; 978922128782, available at: https://www.refworld.org/docid/53999aae4.html [accessed 11 October 2023]

It's not just you!

Compared to the general population, survivors (women involved) in the sex industry experience higher rates of substance abuse, rape, violent assault, sexually transmitted diseases, domestic violence, depression, and post-traumatic stress at rates equivalent to veterans of combat war. Families of the women we serve at Cherished will sometimes come to me and say, "I don't know why she ended up like this."

About 90 percent of children who are victims of sexual abuse know their abuser.[15]

In many situations, trafficking victims – including child victims – know and trust their "first contact" traffickers. Meaning family members, neighbors, boyfriends, friends of the family, and employers.

Many girls are shocked to learn he wasn't really the "boyfriend" or "talent agent" for that modeling job, but that the picture might be much bigger than you knew and you probably weren't the only one he was after. Here is a snapshot of some of the criminal actors involved in human trafficking.

- Individual traffickers: typically operate on their own

- Opportunistic associations of traffickers: two traffickers operating together or more than two traffickers not systematically working together beyond a single crime episode.

- Business-enterprise-type of organized criminal groups: Three or more traffickers systematically working together to traffic persons as a core component of their criminal activities.

15 *Finkelhor, D. (2012). Characteristics of crimes against juveniles. Durham, NH: Crimes against Children Research Center.*

- Governance-type of organized criminal groups: Practice security governance in a community or territory by means of fear and violence and may be involved in multiple illicit markets.[16]

Traffickers have kept pace with technology, becoming adept at using the internet for their trafficking operations. In the early days of the web, they used stand-alone sites before exploiting the potential of classified ad sites and then moving into social media. The internet helps traffickers to operate in multiple locations simultaneously while physically exploiting the victims in just one location.[17]

I **spent ten years** in the commercial **sex industry, being trafficked and exploited** by...

Three different traffickers. They each looked **completely different.**

A friend, A boyfriend, and a colleague.

And they each **were brilliant at grooming.**

From my own experience in this work, I can report 100 percent of the women that I have worked with were abused as children by someone they knew and trusted. And that is where it all started. I have heard countless stories of how they were left with a family member

16 "Global Report on Trafficking in Persons 2020," *UN Office on Drugs and Crime (UNODC)*, Accessed March 29, 2023, https://www.unodc.org/documents/data-and-analysis/tip/2021/ GLOTiP_2020_15jan_web.pdf

17 "Global Report on Trafficking in Persons 2020," *UN Office on Drugs and Crime (UNODC)*, Accessed March 29, 2023, https://www.unodc.org/documents/data-and-analysis/tip/2021/ GLOTiP_2020_15jan_web.pdf

to "watch" them or sold to a family friend. Instead of being in the loving, nurturing, safe care of an adult, they were forced to have sex on a regular basis with a family member or watch porn and then be forced to have sex with a sibling while the abuser watched. This would continue each time the family left them in this person's care, continuing for years.

Abusers often place threats to create fear in the child; sometimes the abuser may threaten to kill their family or pet if they find out and say it will be the child's fault. Or the abuser might threaten to hurt a sibling or parent if the victim ever tells. To a child, these threats are real, and they're a powerful way to silence them from ever telling the truth. Instead of speaking out, victims typically learn to view the abuse they're getting as an indicator of their own low value and lack of worth. Our mission at Cherished is to help women discover their true value and worth. It can take years to undo the shame that a woman experiences because of sexual abuse in her most formative years. Add to that repeated sexual traumas, often including rape and violent sexual assaults, and a survivor's recovery is a lifetime ongoing healing process. Statistics for survivors of the sex industry say that for every year in the industry, there is a five-year recovery. At this rate, I would need the next 50 years to recover from the decade of trauma I had lived through. Add to this the childhood traumas that came before this lifestyle. Considering that and my life as a stripper and escort for over a decade, I'd need the rest of my life to find healing. Many providers still don't diagnose survivors with Complex PTSD because it is not even in the DSM5 (yet), even with all the data we have now, which doesn't aid survivors in making a choice to look for help.

It can take years to undo the shame that a woman experiences because of sexual abuse in her most formative years.

…

As I began working with survivors, I realized I needed to become more skilled at helping the women we serve at Cherished with transformational healing. I enrolled in an intensive training program at the Allender Center that focuses on a specific form of therapy called Narrative Focused Trauma Care. For short, we simply call it Story work. It involves stepping back into your earliest, most formative core memories to grieve what your younger self experienced in times of trauma and reshaping a new narrative—a new story—about how you see yourself. It's a process of replacing lies we've come to believe and agree with about ourselves, especially those that were handed to us unwittingly by neglectful parents, abusers, and others who set out to silence, mar, ruin, steal, kill, or destroy our natural-born inner beauty and innocence.

As I listened to stories from the women in Cherished, I'd hate to hear a girl repeat the words of her pimp: "once a 'ho,' always a ho,'" or "I'm just damaged goods."

I get it! I understand how that feels; like there are no do-overs. My heart breaks. I know the deep pain in those words. They have never had someone tell them they are worthy of love and deserve to see themselves the way God had created them before they were marred by evil. They deserve to discover their true purpose in life. And I have a deep desire to awaken that in them!

That is my passion!

By incorporating Story Groups into our recovery program, I've seen countless women, myself included, experience the deep healing that happens when we shine a light on our shame and trauma. I've watched women receive care from each other as they share their heartbreaking stories, the kind of care they should have received when they were children.

In facilitating these Story Groups and receiving therapy for myself outside of Cherished, I, too, have experienced deep, transformational healing that only happens by rewriting a new narrative about who I am. I am not a false name placed on me like disappointment, problem, addict, prostitute, failure, stupid. But instead, I have discovered that I was created as fierce, stunning, a symbol of purity, a daughter of the highest, a warrior, and a queen.

Whatever your beliefs are, make a proclamation. You are a woman who is __________, __________, and __________.

You are more than what you have been through; you are not what or who they said you were. You are beautifully wild, and it's not too much! It's glorious! You have a purpose!

Opposition will come at you when you make a claim like this, to be sure, but: "Our fight is not with people. It is against the leaders and the powers and the spirits of darkness in this world. It is against the demon world that works in the heavens." (Ephesians 6:12 NLV)

You have been through hell, and you made it out! Don't give up now!

My hope is that now you will be brave once more, but this time for the girl you left behind, the younger you.

Story work or "Narrative Focused Trauma Care" (NFTC) for me was like going back into the shadows to get the girl left a long time ago. It's hard work but worth it when you are ready.

Going back into the shadows
to get the girl left a long time
ago is hard work but worth
it when you are ready.

...

Unfortunately, it's not uncommon for women who leave the sex industry to get caught up in fear of the future before they get to start healing. The unknown can be more terrifying than going back to the abuse; at least it's something familiar, and you know how to navigate those waters. Even romanticizing life from before, missing the abuser. Remembering his care. Longing for his kindness. But kindness is part of the abuser's tactics. It's the web to trap you in.

Many times, this is where you find yourself, on the run going from place to place, unsure of where you belong, not knowing where to land. You're just getting the courage to make a change and wondering what life might be like if you did. But because you can't find safety, you try different places until something goes wrong, or you sabotage it, and then you are on the run again. Staying on the run can feel safer than being still.

In the book, *Pimpology: 48 Laws of the Game*, new pimps learn how to "break a bitch." Wall Street businessmen saw the parallels of how to use techniques from the world of prostitution to gain power in the business world and make their way up the ladder of success: "You have to tear someone's ego down before they start looking to you for salvation. Then you have the chance to build them back up, showing them it's your program that takes them from darkness to hope. Then they will see you as their hero, even if the weakness you rescued them from is the one you created."[18]

When someone I am working with starts to lose perspective and begins to miss and romanticize their old life, I ask a question, which I learned from founder Rachel Lloyd of G.E.M.S., to help survivors remember what they've been through and to process with other survivors the answer to this question, "What don't you miss about being in 'the industry?'"[19]

18 Pimpin' K. & Hunter K. (2008). *Pimpology : the 48 laws of the game* (1st Simon Spotlight Entertainment trade pbk.). Simon & Schuster; Turnaround distributor.

19 Girls Educational & Mentoring Services. (2008). *Very young girls.*

Here are the things I personally don't miss about my old life:

I don't miss… the gut-wrenching feeling I would get when the phone would ring. I would let it ring as many times as I could before I knew I *had* to answer it, all the while wondering what was going to be required of me that day from a club manager, the pimp, the escort service, a John, or the Madam.

I don't miss… walking up to the door of a strange house, whether it be night or day, in Beverly Hills or a hotel room, and wondering who would be on the other side of the door when it opened and what I would be told to do.

I don't miss… waking up and wondering if I might get arrested (again), or raped (again), or if this time it would go too far, and I would be killed!

I don't miss… the feeling of my skin being burned and consumed by men's gaze at first sight of me nude.

I don't miss…getting in a strange bed, trembling, waiting for it to be over.

I don't miss… hoping I make it out of here safely.

I don't miss…being beaten up, tied up, and being powerless under someone else's control.

I don't miss...all the strange smells... smells of darkness and evil.

I don't miss... a client who prematurely ejaculated and then couldn't get an erection again but forced me to continue to find ways to please him because he wanted to use all the time he had paid the pimp for.

I don't miss... being locked in a room and being forced to have sex with multiple men and women while being filmed against my will.

I don't miss... sitting in a bathtub for hours, crying, feeling like I could never get clean enough or scrubbing my skin until it was raw.

I don't miss ...being watched by on-lookers while having sex.

I don't miss...hoping this time it would be a real modeling job interview and not another porn shoot cover-up.

I don't miss... being raped.

I don't miss... being swollen and sore for weeks after being beaten up.

I don't miss... covering up bruises before going out under the stage lights.

I don't miss… straddling some strange man's crotch for a lap dance in a small, box-size room with only a curtain between us and a thousand other people in the club.

I don't miss… dancing nude for single dollar bills on a stage.

I don't miss… working for mafia (club owners) and having my life threatened if I refuse to have sex with their VIP clients.

I don't miss…dirty dressing rooms.

I don't miss… being kicked out of moving cars.

I don't miss… having my hair pulled.

I don't miss… being homeless and staying with men I couldn't stand and letting them grope me just to stay off the streets.

I don't miss… entering a strange place and scanning the room for cameras and wondering if I was secretly being videotaped.

I don't miss…men with their sick fetishes, who wanted to be hurt with my stilettos, or powdered and nursed like a baby, or wanting golden showers, or being forced into bondage, tied up and locked up, and being threatened with how they could leave me to die if they wanted to.

I don't miss… being afraid for my life because I was told by a stranger that they wanted to rape me.

I don't miss… being strangled.

I don't miss… being locked in a hotel room for two days and not knowing if I was going to live or if anyone would find me.

I don't miss… being stalked by psychos, who saw me naked on stage then waited for me in the parking lots and attacked me.

I don't miss… having to give a cop a blow job to get out of being arrested.

I don't miss… being locked up in a women's prison and not being able to eat because someone spit in my food.

Just to name a few that I don't miss.

These may all be in the past now, but the triggers can sometimes still interfere with my focus and the way I process the lens I see people through. That's one of the core symptoms of PTSD.

Part of my own healing process comes from helping others escape from all the things they don't miss, either. Together, we're building lives based on a vision for a more positive future, one that leaves space for us to love ourselves and live lives of purpose and meaning and joy.

QUESTIONS: GOING UPSTREAM

1. Who was your first abuser? Was it someone you trusted?

2. What are the things you don't miss about the lifestyle you had before? If you still haven't made that decision, what are some things you wouldn't miss that you have to do now?

3. Take some time to write them down. How do you feel about this list?

CHAPTER 26

CHERISHED

"The flashbacks are a constant reminder
that the nightmare was real."

· · ·

There are so many more stories about being in the sex industry that I have not put in this book. What I've shared here are just a few from more than a decade's worth, and these took over 20 years to heal from to be mentally ready to finish this book. There is so much I have learned and much more I want to say, but it would require another few books to share it all. In the meantime, I am going to keep growing and learning and healing, because that is how it is meant to be.

Maya Angelou said her grandmother told her, "If you get something, give something. If you learn something, teach something". Those are life lessons.

I gained so much from all I have been through; I've grown and healed, and I want to pass it on so others can find their purpose.

God had given me a call on my life that started the day I walked out of the club in 1994. And it was terrifying to think of doing it, but I almost died in that life! I couldn't just walk away, leaving others like me to face the same trauma all alone after leaving like I had to.

I couldn't just walk away,
leaving others like me to face
the same trauma all alone
after leaving like I had to.

• • •

I have heard other survivors repeat similar stories; sometimes, it's like they are telling me my own story. It is vital in the anti-trafficking movement to have a survivor-led program or at least a survivor leader on staff, LEADING. Survivors need a sherpa who has been this way before and knows the terrain.

When I have the privilege to sit with women in their trauma stories, I consider it sacred ground that we are on because I know how hard it is to allow someone into my stories of harm. I feel it is an honor and privilege to be trusted.

It is so healing to have a witness to your stories, someone who won't turn their face away or try to minimize your pain because it's too much to hold. Although I believe most people are unaware of it, they have been conditioned and don't realize what they are doing when they do it.

Saying things that are not helpful but are more about making the person saying it feel better minimizes the storyteller's pain. It isn't always beneficial to share scripture in moments when someone is sharing their story. When no one has been able to name the physiological chains and help you see them, you will continue to reenact the abuse repeatedly. What a survivor needs is for you to grieve with them over their loss; instead of trying to rescue them from pain, try to sit with them. Even the bible tells Christians to mourn with those who mourn and rejoice with those who rejoice. Meaning, to be present.

> ## What a survivor needs is for you to grieve with them over their loss; instead of trying to rescue them from pain, try to sit with them.

...

If someone is saying something that takes you away from your story when you are sharing, recognize that if they are trying to "make you feel better," it's more for their own relief. I have watched this happen so many times, and it really is about the person offering the rescue. They have not done enough work healing from their own pain to be comfortable with yours. Or they may bring up their own story to try to relate to yours, which is often another form of diversion when feeling uncomfortable. Or they may get angry and compare traumas; this is the biggest sign someone isn't safe for you. It is why it is so essential for people to do their own healing (story) work and understand their own attachment styles before helping someone else. You need to know how you are going to show up and what will trigger you. (See the attachment styles in the back of this book.)

I didn't have a safe space to tell my story so that I could begin to assemble a cohesive narrative that helps my body to release trauma and heal. Instead, I spent almost 20 years alone suffering from Complex PTSD.

With nowhere to go with it.

There are many books and articles on the brain and trauma and trauma in the body. *The Body Keeps Score, Healing Trauma,* and *Releasing the Tiger* are a few good ones.

All of those years I worked in strip clubs as an exotic dancer and then as an escort, money was easy to come by. I knew what to do and who to get it from. But most of the time, I was miserable and depressed, and my body was always on high alert and in a constant state of flight or fight or freeze for survival. Although I experienced the instant gratification of making money, every time I traded sex for dollars, a piece of me died, and I became even more fragmented.

When I felt the time was right, and I started sharing my vision of Cherished, I had no idea how people would react, but I knew no matter what they said, I HAD to do it.

Some encouraged me and thought I was brave, realizing the need, but had no interest in helping me out. I was also met with some discouragement and doubt by people who thought these women get what they want and deserve. And some found it fascinating, like a sexy ministry, which can be voyeuristic.

There were all kinds of reasons and judgments coming against me. Some argued I would be "silly to do so because women chose this life." But don't let anyone else's fear stop you when you feel so strongly about something.

The naysayers will always be there. Please don't fall for it. It's usually because something about you stepping into your call is a threat to them. I look at it as a sign that I am doing something right. The cost of not stepping into your calling is far greater.

I knew it wasn't about whether or not I had all of the knowledge I needed to run a nonprofit—those things can be learned, and great people can be found who can do the day-to-day.

But what can't be learned or hired is having the experience of living through something that dark and getting out alive. Offering that kind of hope can only come from a lived experience.

In her book, *Redeeming Heartache*, founder Cathy Loerzel writes, "When a queen is decisive, the rest of the kingdom can relax and reorient…However, her leadership exposes her to either adulation or criticism…she is likely to be cast as a hero or a villain. This can be a setup for grandiosity or devaluation, depending on the outcome of the decision."[20]

How true those words are. Many have tried to devalue my role, but those same people have never been in my (or your) shoes. So, they can try as they may, but everyone has their place and calling, and no one can take away yours or vice versa.

Helping women discover their purpose and find freedom *is* my calling and purpose. And 1000X, I'd say yes again. (Contact me if you are called to start something like this. I have so much more to say. So many things I wish I had known.)

You will need help to prepare for what it means to hold the weight of success or failure, which can be very hard. Especially when working with women who don't trust anyone, there is a lot at stake if you fail them (and you will sometimes fail—but rupture and repair are part of the work).

Training the staff and volunteers for this work was another piece that would prove super challenging. Working with survivors is very

20 Allender D. B. & Loerzel C. (2021). *Redeeming heartach : how past suffering reveals our true calling.* Zondervan.

emotional, and not everyone can hold these kinds of trauma stories, especially (I keep saying this because it is so vitally important) if they have not worked on their own stories of harm.

People are drawn to help others for many reasons; they want to "give back" because they have been in a place where they needed help and are grateful for someone helping them, or they are trying to rescue themselves (because no one was there for them). Either way, as soon as we start diving into the trauma a survivor endures, people start disappearing and dropping like flies. They don't keep their commitments or start trying to go rogue, taking things in a different direction, and running their own program, deciding what is best.

In my experience, the girls have come to Cherished because they trusted another survivor to lead and show them the way.

Dan Allender, author, and therapist, said it best: "You can only take people as far as you have gone yourself." This work is hard, and it's not for everyone.

Over these years, there have been some fantastic people that have teamed up with me; they give me hope that I don't have to do this alone and that there are people out there who want to go the distance. Those are great times; when you find them, it is a gift! If you can find someone who can take your vision, run with it, stay on track, and help you grow, you have hit the jackpot!

I have an excellent Director, Kayla, who has been with me for years. She came to me right after graduating from Bible college. I thought, *NO WAY, these girls will destroy her; she will never last here.* But I am happy to say she accepted the challenge (it is why we work so well together); she has taken my vision as her own and has used her gifts to strengthen and grow Cherished. That was the favor of God! You can't do work like this being a lone wolf. You need like-minded people who will support you and work with you, not against you.

I have also experienced those who come along to "help," and because they have leadership skills, they believe you should turn over the reins. And then there are some to come along who want to "to get involved," but what they really want is to redirect the whole ship.

Be aware: envy is stealthy and often shows up through the people you least expect. There have been times when I thought someone was a friend but instead was hurt by their envy, which always caught me by surprise. It would immediately trigger that familiar feeling of betrayal. And for me, self-contempt isn't very far behind betrayal. I can start believing something is wrong with me. I could spiral out if I'm not careful. Becoming depressed and/or hyper-vigilant. When that happens, the first step I must take is tending to my heart. This is where understanding your whole story comes in. I cannot say enough about how important it is to have a therapist that is trained in C-PTSD to help you. Understanding your style of relating is very important, which comes from your family of origin, then add all your sexual abuse from being in the industry! It's A LOT!

(My therapist wrote the forward, but in the back of this book, there are many I trust who could lead you to someone who they recommend.)

For years I would go into this spiral, and when it would happen, I would be confused, and in shock, but then as I started healing and getting free, seeing who God made me to be and stepping into more of who I am, I began to realize that envy is more about the person feeling threatened; something comes up for them and exposes something of their heart toward themselves (which goes back to their own self-contempt).

In a healthy relationship, there can be a place to address this, and growth and repair for both can happen, but unfortunately, that is not always the case.

When you have functioned in a world of scandal and backstabbing, you learn to read the room well. You know when something is toxic, and to survive you've learned how to navigate it if circumstances require it. But when you start to heal, you begin to walk away from toxic people and situations instead of trying to survive them.

> # When you start to heal, you begin to walk away from toxic people and situations instead of trying to survive them.
>
> ...

When you begin to find out who you are, what you are meant to do, and where your place in the world is, then there will always be those who think you don't deserve ________ (fill in the blank). But they don't know what you have been through and why you are where you are, why God chose you!

When I started learning to lead (and I really worked hard at it, full time, reading books, taking training, and talking with mentors and counselors), there always seemed to be someone whispering that they could "do it better;" and in some areas, they totally could. But now in those moments, I remind myself they weren't given to steward what I was. God knew exactly what he was getting when he chose me. He's not shocked or surprised by my failures and mistakes. It's humbling, and it causes me to lean in even more, to remind me of who I am, and to listen for his wisdom and instruction. Our biggest calling comes from our deepest pain. And many will be restored when we say yes, SO I will keep dreaming and keep pushing the envelope.

In the years since the first retreat where we introduced our healing oil, "Hadassah," I felt like it was a treasure straight from heaven for women. We burn this oil in the studio to create a calm atmosphere. We've expanded and created an entire line of bath and body products around it, along with handcrafted jewelry and some apparel designed by survivors. By employing Cherished women to help make the products and run this social enterprise, we can offer meaningful, safe work to women in our program. We also provide rent-free housing for a year while working on their recovery. Bit by bit, we've been able to make more services and resources available to an increasing number of women from all over the US through Cherished.

One of the first things I noticed about myself was when I realized how difficult the fundraising aspect of running this nonprofit would be.

This was for several reasons.

Being raised in the South, I was taught that it was vulgar and shameful to talk about money, especially in public. That is still a part of who I am. Then in the commercial sex industry, money reflects a person's (my) value and worth.

And the second, perhaps even the more significant reason—the familiar feeling of performing for it, being "good enough" to be chosen, seen as "worthy" enough for someone to give their money to—it feels transactional. It puts me back in that bind, no matter how you spin it.

And it frustrates me that I have to "sell" to another human being the idea we should do something about human trafficking.

At first, there was NO government funding, and I had to rely solely on donations. So, it was my job then, as it is for any executive director, to fundraise to keep things going.

But as someone who has been exploited and treated as a commodity, this is a huge trigger. I realized that if I wanted to help other women, I would have to go back out there on "that stage" (get in front of crowds) and exploit myself (tell my story) to get it.

The most effective way to capture the hearts and minds of donors is by sharing my own and others' experiences in the sex industry, and if often feels voyeuristic. Relying on others for financial support is a powerless and familiar feeling.

I'm committed to growing Cherished and preserving it as a safe place for women to recover from their life in the sex industry. It is my love of casting a vision for why CherishedLA is an organization worth supporting that helps me push through my sense of fear and discomfort in raising money. The women we serve are beyond worth it!

When I'm asked to speak, whether in a boardroom or at a huge fundraising event, I never want to invite people to be voyeurs, and yet you can't understand the magnitude of the damage that's done in the sex industry unless you hear the stories about women whose lives have been destroyed through exploitation.

It would be easier if I could tell the story of widespread sexual exploitation and modern-day sex trafficking in a tidy PowerPoint of graphs and stats. But numbers alone don't paint the picture of what is happening to us. Numbers don't show the grit for why Cherished needs to exist and how we help transform women's lives. Numbers actually keep the humanity out of it, in a place where everything can be kept in the margins at a value-seeking level—which is the whole story of the industry itself. My life and the hell I have experienced are not something that can be understood in a graph.

When someone chooses to "look the other way," they are choosing to justify the demand that fuels the industry. So when someone says don't take it personally, it is like a punch in the gut.

Yes, it is personal for me. Staying alive was very personal! And now someone else's daughter needs me to make it personal.

Relying on others to hear me, to understand that this is serious, and we need to help women get free; laying all of my pain out before them, sharing about something I have poured all of me into to help another soul and wondering constantly if someone will give so that this will survive long enough to help the next girl who calls; it's a constant setup to face betrayal and powerlessness, repeatedly.

At one event where I spoke, even after explaining the direct correlation between childhood abuse and exploitation, a man said to me, "Women do this because it's what they want. It's empowering, and there is nothing wrong with it."

I'm shocked that I always have to de-bunk the myths that women in the sex industry are there because "they wanted it" or that "it's empowering," No, sir, this is not why women work in the sex industry. His statement implied that the sexual trauma that I and others have suffered isn't real, that we wanted sexual abuse, and that we were complicit and empowered in selling ourselves for money. I have encountered more narcissistic clients than I can count, who deny the reality of human trafficking and dismiss the victim as a scapegoat to hide their own insatiable lust; this is why people say and think these things. I am Exposing it. The only way they can feel relief from accountability for the problem is to distance themselves from their own shame.

But for the rest of us who have experienced the pain and suffering of sexual exploitation, we understand that this kind of ignorance makes it easy for traffickers to move about with their prey right under your nose and fuels the demand. The real conspiracy, the real gaslighting, is happening to those who fall for it. Unfortunately, people are deceived into believing there is nothing happening. Instead of fighting for the rights of another human, they have become accomplices.

We don't live in a society that acknowledges the trauma that the sex industry creates. "Empowering" may feel true at first. Because after being abused, it does feel empowering to be the one in control for a change, to call the shots, especially after someone has been forced to be the submissive to an abuser like a "John," pimp, brother, father, or uncle. Taking back control and being the one who seduces instead of being the one trapped by a predator feels like empowerment.

Evil comes to steal both overtly and covertly. And the trauma doesn't differentiate between the two. Choice or Force. It's still going to get you. One day the reality will set in, and you will realize that the flashbacks are a reminder that it was real.

If I haven't been clear about the word "choice" and what that really means to someone who has been sexually abused, then let me give you this quote by Dan Allender, an expert in trauma: "You can't disconnect the context in which the choice was made, homelessness or prostitution. Survival is a necessities decision! You cannot know what rendered them so vulnerable to be in survival …no less violence is suffered."[21]

I have left many meetings, got into my car, closed the door, and screamed, letting the tears flow.

21 Allender D. B. & Loerzel C. (2021). *Redeeming heartache: how past suffering reveals our true calling.* Zondervan.

When will people start to see that a life in the sex industry is not a true choice? Almost every woman I have worked with has suffered some form of sexual abuse as a child. When a child is sexually abused, the trauma is embedded in the subconscious. It doesn't just go away.

The sex industry validates their feelings of worthlessness. For some, it can feel empowering, at least for a season, because it seems to take back the power, to have control over men (AKA their abuser). But no one escapes the trauma left in the wake of sexual abuse and exploitation.

NO ONE!

More times than I can count, I was forced to "work" a few days around major sporting events and hired to escort and attend many events and pro games with someone that needed me to stroke his fragile ego. This book shares just a few examples of flashbacks and nightmares many live with. I often feel the double-bind of helping women out of sexual slavery and raising money from the very people who keep the cycle of abuse alive. As hard as fundraising can sometimes be, I am still committed to raising awareness about the issue of sexual exploitation and sex trafficking.

I am committed to raising the funds needed to provide a safe place and restore women so that they can freely choose the kind of life they want to live. I am committed to flinging open the cage doors so that women can fly free.

If ALL of these efforts were to only save ONE life, I'm in! It's that serious! SHE IS WORTH IT!

QUESTIONS: CHERISHED

True freedom is not sweeping things under the rug and saying, "I forgive" just so things can feel fine. You'll end up tripping over all those lumps under the rug! When we struggle with self-hate and self-contempt, guilt and trauma still hold us hostage. The greatest healing I have found is walking through the process of narrative trauma work with experts on sexual harm. (You'll find resources at the end of this book.)

1. Do you have moments when your past comes up and still triggers you today? This can be a sign that you still have healing to do.

Here is a poem written by a stunning woman who I am so proud of. She is truly the definition of what it means to be a survivor, overcomer, and now a liberator.

With HIS love She will be fearless

She will move mountains in the distance

In this home She will be shown kindness

And learn within her there is Goodness

With help She will get healing

Whatever was lost will be restored

She came here scared but willing

By HIM She is adored

With her story She will reach others

Who had a life like Hers

Spreading Hope to Her Sisters and Brothers

So They all can change the world

In the Word She will find Freedom

Peace, Love, and Mercy

She will be welcomed in HIS Kingdom

And Guaranteed Victory

In the night I will look upon the stars

And make a simple wish

No matter where she and I are

We will remember We are Cherished

*** DEDICATED TO: ALL CHERISHED WOMEN***

Written by Kanisha R. Hamilton

CHAPTER 27

AN EMPTY CAGE

"At first, they were unaware that the door had
been opened for them and they were free to fly."

. . .

66 I sat in the backstage dressing room at the strip club, getting ready for my next set. I knew if I didn't make enough at the club, I would have to take "calls." I wondered if tonight would be worth the effort or just another night lost in time. How long would I have to do this before I got what I came to LA for? Staring at my face in the mirror, looking deep into my eyes. Wondering if any part of that young girl was still there?"

Those days are behind me now. It took incredible strength to survive a day in that lifestyle; it was a very traumatic experience. Looking back now, I can see how those beautiful white doves I kept all those years grounded me and brought me back. Like in Inception, the birds were my "totem" separating me from the madness that was my life, and making my hardened heart have "feeling" again.

Many years later, when I finally got away from "the industry," I moved away from Hollywood to put some separation between my past and me. I wanted to disappear so no one could find, use, or hurt me again. For a long time, I wanted to be invisible. I ran to the desert, where I felt safe. It was quieter, and I could be alone. One day I was sitting looking at those same birds and thinking about all I had survived and how thankful I was to be free from it all. Suddenly it occurred to me: I was free, but my beloved doves were still in captivity. They had kept me company all these years. And they had kept something alive in me—the desire to be free.

I picked up the four-foot white antique cage and carried them outside. Opening the door to the cage, I sat down on the ground beside it; they were looking up, staring right into my eyes like they knew it was our final moment together.

"Thank you," I whispered, "but now it's your turn to be free!" After a few minutes, they found the opening and flew out. One flew into my lap and looked at me as if she was thanking me; she cooed one last time and then took flight.

It felt like such a sacred moment.

I sat there watching them, discovering that they were free now as tears welled up from a deep place; I'm sure the tears were about more than saying goodbye to my feathered friends; I was mourning for the girl who had come here with so much hope and for all the harm she had endured. This was the end of it. We were finally free. I was not sure what was next for me.

I kept those empty cages that I had collected over the years for a long time. I left them around my house with the doors flung open as a reminder that I was free.

I knew that, somewhere, those birds were thankful, too.

QUESTIONS: AN EMPTY CAGE

Sometimes creating a ceremony or a ritual can help mark an important decision or turning point in our lives. I have thrown rocks with words written in them out into the deep ocean or painted rocks and placed them to mark an important place. (Heather Stringer is a creative and gifted therapist and has a lot of information about the importance of creating rituals for yourself. Check out lifeinritual.com)

1. What makes your heart sing? You have a gift and a passion that is different from every human on this earth. Answer that, and then fiercely step into it.

RESOURCES

To learn more about healing from the trauma of exploitation, sexual harm, and abuse, the following are just a few of my favorite resources.

Books

Healing the Wounded Heart by Dan Allender

To Be Told by Dan Allender

Redeeming Heartache by Dan Allender and Cathy Loerzel

Healing Trauma by Peter Levine

The Wisdom of Your Body by Hillary L. McBride

Unwanted by Jay Stringer

My Grandmother's Hands by Resmaa Menakem

In An Unspoken Voice by Peter Levine

Waking The Tiger by Peter Levine

The Body Keeps the Score by Bessel van der Kolk

Safe People by Henry Cloud and John Townsend

Boundaries by Henry Cloud and John Townsend

Trauma-Informed Yoga: A Toolbox for Therapists: 47 Practices to Calm Balance, and Restore the Nervous System by Joanne Spence and Amy Weintraub

Recovery from Narcissistic Abuse, Gaslighting, Codependency and Complex PTSD (4 Books in 1) by Linda Hill

Impacts Of Childhood Trauma: Basic Knowledge Of Psychological Trauma: Effects Of Childhood Trauma On Brain Development by Randell Ji

Adult Children of Emotionally Immature Parents by Lindsay Gibson

What Happened to You?: Conversations on Trauma, Resilience, and Healing by Oprah Winfrey, Bruce D. Perry, et al.

Podcasts

The Place We Find Ourselves, by Adam Young

The Allender Center Podcast, by Dan Allender

"Notice the Rage, Notice the Silence" with Krista Tippett and Resmaa Menakem, On Being

"The Story Behind Pornography Use" with Jay Stringer on Leading Saints podcast, November 27, 2021

"The Whys Behind Pornography" with Jay Stringer on Hole in My Heart with Laurie Krieg, episode 57

"How Sexual Brokenness Reveals Our Way to Healing" with Jay Stringer on Christian Sexuality podcast, episode 2

Trauma Recovery Training Programs

Art of Living Counseling: artoflivingcounseling.com

Adam Young: adamyoungcounseling.com

Allender Center: theallendercenter.org

Jay Stringer:

> The Sexual Attachment Conference: www.sexualattachment.com

> Journey Course- www.journeycourse.com

If you are looking for more resources, visit our website www.cherishedla.org or reach out!

ACKNOWLEDGMENTS ABOUT THIS JOURNEY

Of all the pages in this book, these were the hardest to write. When I need words the most, they fail me. Forgive me.

To the one who's love never fails,

I know without a doubt if not for God I would not be alive today!

From a very young age He became my one and only Father. I can see now, He was there through it all, no matter what decisions I made. He never took his eyes off of me and I have always been on His heart. "He rescued me because he delighted in me" (Psalm 18:19). And now I am keeping my eyes on Him.

To my Mother, a prayer warrior.

If I could talk to you once more, I would want to say this...

As a child, you taught me about God's love and how to pray. I've never forgotten that, even in the darkest of times. Even though you didn't know where I was or what was happening to me, I have no doubt your late-night petitions before God were what spared my life more than once. Thank you for never giving up and for continuing to pray!

I know the greatest joy for you now would be to know that the prayers you prayed on behalf of your grandchildren and great-grandchildren have been answered.

"Tell your children about it (God's provision), and let your children tell their children, and their children the next generation" Joel 1:3

To my three children, Ellie, Adelyne, and Levi,

YOU have been my greatest JOY and HEALING!

I know many people who would never let their children know what mistakes they have made in their past for fear it would give them license to stumble.

Instead, I have watched you love deeper, grow wiser, and stand stronger in who you were created to be. Watching you become YOU has been stunning! We have had many deep conversations, tears, and laughter. Thank you for always encouraging and supporting the work to heal and to help others, even though the cost was high.

I am amazed, still, that God chose me to be your mother. It has been my honor and delight. You are my dearest, proudest moments for as long as I live.

I love you all to the moon and back, x infinity. Mom

To my friend, Karen Fish,

You have seen it all! If not for you, I'm not sure I would have remained sane.

We have laughed until we couldn't breathe and solved the problems of the world. How those time have been medicine for me. You've always spoken the truth to me and I love you for it. There were many dark hours and tears through this process, crying out to God and feeling completely and utterly alone over these years. But you were there to remind me I was not. You have always pointed me back to the Father. You have been there for me through some of those darkest times. You have offered beautiful sage wisdom always with kindness. You have cried on my behalf and loved me through it all. You saw me in the trenches and held a lantern on my dark pathway so I could keep going. I'm eternally grateful for your love and friendship!

To Pastor Mark Goodell,

You were the first to fully support my calling to start Cherished. You have always had my back and been there to listen, pray, and advise me. Thank you for always encouraging me and supporting the work of Cherished. Thank you for showing me what a humble and honest man looks like. I never tire of your reminders that you care; "Have I told you lately"? Love you!

To Harmony Dust,

Thank you for leading the way. You have given me strength to become a liberator. Without your example, I don't know if I would have stepped into this work. God knew and set me up to meet you. I will always treasure our work together in LA, Vegas, Brazil, New York— and the adventure continues to this day! I am so honored to call you friend and mentor.

To Chris Flynn,

When I first met you, I knew you were my kind of person. You had me at (from the moment you ate the fried crickets) "no box needed." HAHA!

And immediately, I was like YEP! Your laughter during our crazy talks and our fun adventures is contagious. Through our stories we have shared secrets, walked through some dark places together, and laughed until we cried. You have offered me safe spaces to be myself and truth and kindness with some of the best insight I have heard. That comes from understanding your own pain and healing. Thank you for being a safe space in friendship and for reading through this book a few times. I am humbled and so grateful to call you friend!

Love you!

To Rhonda Reynolds,

You are a person with insight and wisdom. A Sage. You "see" well and have a way with words that I admire. Anyone who can call you their friend has found a real treasure here on earth. You were the first to read my book OUT LOUD to me (and Chris). That was the best gift (and so timely of a girl's weekend) that I could have asked for. Your kindness and offering were more healing for me than you could ever know. The best medicine anyone could ask for is to have a friend to both go to the depths to laugh so hard with that they almost pee in their pants. (I'm not saying anyone did.) Thank you for always picking up the phone for those long conversations. You are a gift; I am so honored and blessed by your friendship! Love you!

To Trapper Lukaart,

Thank you for meeting with me that day! I was so nervous and unsure if I could ever open up my pandoras box to anyone. But you were never fazed. I felt the support I had never known. You were an answer to prayer. Thank you for seeing me and walking me through this healing process. I never thought that was even possible to trust another human to hold all "my stuff." You have shown me safety, respect, and kindness, and even made me love all that I am, even the crazy parts. Thank you for naming me how you have. Thank you for writing my Foreword. I will treasure that always. My hope would be for everyone to find someone like you to help them discover the wonder of who they were created to be. Forever grateful!

To Cory James,

Thank you for believing in me from the moment we met. I am in awe of your talents and gifts! You truly do offer words of hope. I am so grateful to you for your willingness to invest time, talents, and resources to kick start the publishing process for this book and for using your skills with the cover. I am excited for other projects to come! Thank you for the encouragement. You made this finally happen! I thank God for you. His plans are the best!

To my niece, Martha McQuaid,

Thank you for loving your crazy Aunt no matter what they said. You saw more. Thank you for all the ways you helped me with this project (proofreading, social media) and for writing a beautiful synopsis of this book. You are a beautiful spirit and have so much to offer this world. I am very proud to call you family. I love you!

To Joel Cudworth,

I love you more than my luggage! I can't tell you what it means after all these years to be reunited. I prayed for it! I love you and will always treasure every moment we get together! You are some of the BEST memories of my life. I Love you!!

To Roe Dodgen,

Thank you for being a mentor in my life and friend over these years. Thank you for introducing me to a deeper healing, and for teaching me how to offer more to the women I serve. Thank you for reading this book while still in the working stages and offering me your support and kind words. I am forever grateful for all you have taught me. Deep gratitude!

To Natalie Sum,

Thank you for being such a safe person, for me and the ladies at Cherished. I had never shared my written book with anyone; I was so afraid to take that step but you made me feel safe to give it a try and you introduced me to my first editor. Thank you for giving me courage. We all love you!

To Rachel Clinton Chen, heart healer,

You were the first to offer care for some of these stories. You showed me the tender tears of a mother's heart that I had never known. I am forever grateful for your kindness and fierceness! My deepest gratitude always.

To Marian Liautaud, my very first editor.

This book has been re-written a few times since those beginning days when we were going through edits, but boy, did I learn a lot from you. Thank you for not running when I said "my whole life has been edited; edit me, but don't edit me." You were patient with me. Thank you for your kindness.

You taught me how to turn my words into a book!

*To Eland Mann at Conversation Publishing and
George Stevens at G Sharp Design,*

Thank you for seeing me in this book and making sure my voice was heard. You did a fantastic job in every way! Thank you for your patience with me and for treating this book with dignity and respect.

To Angela and Kanisha,

Fierce and kind. You are the reason for Cherished. Your lives are a testimony to God's goodness. You have come full circle and are now walking with women on their recovery healing journey. You are true leaders. I've prayed so long for you! I could not feel more proud of all the hard work you've done, it's absolutely stunning.

To Kayla Campbell,

I could have never imagined when I started this work how the story would evolve. I am so grateful God sent you to walk with me to be my confidant.

You have shown love and support for me personally and for the women and vision of Cherished. It's so fun doing this "life" (instead of "work") together. I am in awe. I did not think it possible for someone to step up and have as much passion for this as I do. But you surpass all I could ask for; and the way you face our many, many challenges, its amazing! It's been a fantastic voyage, even if we are building the ship while at sea! LOL. I love our adventures together (hey, at least we turned in the keys!).

You have embraced this vision and walked so close with me as a friend. It's truly stunning! This work is heavy and heartbreaking but you have stayed for it. Two are stronger than one and together we have been able stand to make a difference. I love your fierce "we got this" spirit; you always cheer us on and encourage me to keep going.

I could never express here in a few words the depth of kindness, the beauty, and the healing you have brought to me throughout the years. The love and support you have offered me has been a gift. You may never truly know on this side of heaven what you have done for me. You are truly CHERISHED!! I love you girl!

To all the women who have come to Cherished for healing,

You are my sisters; this is for you and I am always going to be for you. You are the bravest, strongest women I know, and I am so proud of you! Through our healing together, we have laughed and cried. I have shared with you things that are not even in this book. I love you all!

I hope you never again forget who you are. Daughters of the one true KING of Kings.

To all the staff, interns, and volunteers who have been a part of this work over the years,

Each of you has played a significant role in Cherished, so that I could get the healing I needed and finish writing this book. Thank you for loving the women and for trusting me.

To anyone I have missed,

I truly apologize. These acknowledgements have been about those who have walked closely with me through the process of writing this book and of healing from the trauma of my past. But it's not the complete journey of Cherished. I am still on this journey and there is probably another book to come.

Stay Tuned.

MORE FROM KATE AND CHERISHED

CherishedLA offers hope and healing to survivors of sexual exploitation and human trafficking with (survivor-led) support groups, residential programs, employment, education, and outreach.

If you or someone you know is stuck in a life of sexual exploitation or suffering from the effects of it and looking for a way out, CherishedLA is a non-judgmental community that knows what it's like. We are here when you are ready.

If you need help, someone is here for you, please reach out!

Email: kate@cherishedla.org

To Join Kate in a Trauma Focused Story Workshops group

Kate has 7 years of training and certificates in leading trauma workshops and has been leading survivors' support groups for over a decade. She knows how to offer the care you deserve for your story and help you find healing.

Email: kate@cherishedla.org

Visit Us Online:

Website: www.cherishedla.org

Instagram | @CherishedLA

Facebook | @CherishedLA

Please consider supporting CherishedLA financially.

We can't do it without you!

www.cherishedla.org/donate

If you would like to book Kate to speak at your event:

www.cherishedla.org/kate-wedell

www.ingramcontent.com/pod-product-compliance
Lightning Source LLC
Chambersburg PA
CBHW051221130726
47988CB00001B/164